Nelson

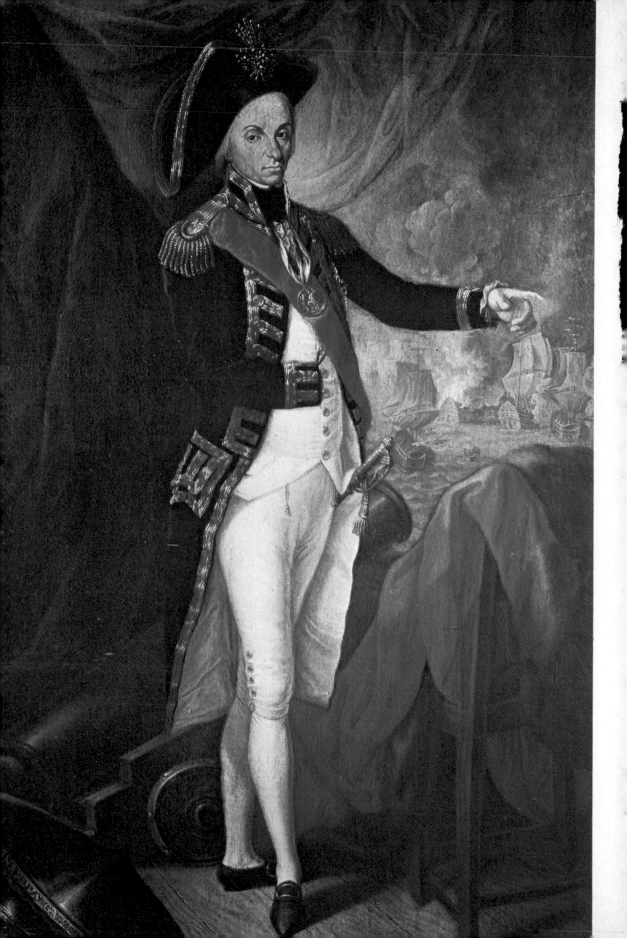

Nelson

Oliver Warner

Introduction by Elizabeth Longford

Follett Publishing Company Chicago

First published in the
United States of America
1975 by
Follett Publishing Company,
Chicago

ISBN 0–695–80541–X
Library of Congress Catalog Card Number 74–21370

Printed in England

House editor Enid Gordon
Art editor Tim Higgins
Layout by Sheila Sherwen
Picture research Pat Hodgson

Dedicated to
Lily McCarthy
who, with her husband John
has done so much to keep
fresh the memory of Nelson

Contents

THE VICTORY

BRITONS!
Your NELSON is dea[d]
Trust not in an Arm of Fles[h]
in the *Living GOD!*
WHAT SAID THE BRA[VE]
Nelson, Duncan,
ath given us the V IC
is not cold in
ened that it cannot
BRITONS
GOD, Fear SIN, An[d]
Fear Nothing

Horatia

"NELSON"
Cast from Nature after his death
on board the "VICTORY."

Introduction

THE NELSON TOUCH is a phrase synonymous with greatness. Yet many people would hesitate to define its exact meaning. There is obviously Nelson's overall genius as an admiral. Beyond that, we think of momentous occasions when he applied his touch. On joining the fleet before Trafalgar, for instance, he himself said 'the *Nelson Touch*' sent a thrill of confidence like an electric shock through all his ships. There is also his inimitable way with words, unequalled in wartime until Churchill. 'England expects. . . .' Again, many will always see more than a touch of poetry in his poignant love-story. Not least, there was his famous charisma. That overworked term should be reserved for Nelson alone. It might have been made for him. At his funeral, his friend, the Reverend Dr Scott, traced some of the elements in his personal charm: 'When I think, setting aside the heroism, what an affectionate fascinating little fellow he was, how dignified and pure his mind, how kind and condescending his manners, I become stupid with grief for what I have lost'.

This is a fresh assessment of England's most popular hero by the distinguished naval historian, whose ancestor, Dr Warner, was one of those surgeons who examined the stump of Nelson's arm, for a pension. Oliver Warner gives us many quotations from newly available material, and the 'touch' is analysed for us through exciting adventure and lucid commentary. But in the last resort, that 'something' which made Nelson different from all other heroes is shown by the author to be indefinable, since Nelson was 'individual in so many ways.'

Impressive background detail helps to build up the picture. 'I have tried to assess', writes Oliver Warner, 'how much Nelson was a man of his time.' Courtesy between enemies is seen to be a custom of that age which might well have been longer preserved. Nelson's tribute to the 'Brave Danes' at Copenhagen compares favourably with the resentment expressed when Churchill paid a similar compliment to Rommel. Over physical punishments, however, the record is reversed. Nelson's victories cannot be separated from the horrors of naval discipline. His uninhibited

6

acceptance of brutal practices provokes a question. Why did Wellington, because he 'put in the boot', so to speak, in the Army, go down to history unfairly as an Iron Duke, whereas the stigma of an equally savage Navy did not stick to Nelson? Part of the answer must lie in yet another attribute of the 'Nelson touch' which Oliver Warner emphasizes.

Admiral Lord Nelson took his captains into his confidence. They were his 'Band of Brothers'. Such an atmosphere of friendship could not but percolate through the whole Navy, doing much to dispel the evil effects of barbarity and the press gang.

The hero had faults which his biographer does not conceal. But it is the admiral himself who is the first to point them out. 'I am hasty', he wrote; and, 'Figure to yourself a vain man. . . .' Such candour was irresistible, springing as it did from a God-fearing nature. The 'fascinating little fellow' of 1805 quickly became Britain's tutelary deity. This state of things had its dangers for the Navy, as Oliver Warner shows in his moving last chapter. Nevertheless the worship accorded to Nelson was both inevitable and splendidly deserved. For he won not only battles but hearts.

Elizabeth Longford

Foreword

SOME EXPLANATION may seem fitting, from one who has already written much about Nelson, for the appearance of this new book. If he is studied at all extensively, Nelson is likely to become a life-long preoccupation. The case is the same with most people of genius, even when their gifts have been applied to war and thus, to some inevitable degree, to destruction.

My own interest in the admiral dates from childhood. I grew up at my mother's home at Beccles, in Suffolk, a town which has always been proud of its associations with Nelson, for his parents courted there, and in 1749 they were married in the splendid Perpendicular church, where Nelson's father had served as a curate. Years later, when the country had news of the sea victory over the French in Aboukir Bay, Beccles celebrated by ringing peals in the bell-tower. John Gowing, one of the ringers, kept a diary in which he noted: '1798 October. Great news from Horatio Nelson, who took nine ships of the line. Wringing.' In those days, news took time to travel, but its impact was far greater than it could be today, when it arrives continuously. 'Wringing' recurred in an entry for 5 December 1805, when Beccles heard about Trafalgar. This time, since the nation had to mourn Nelson, Gowing's quaint spelling was sadly apt.

A Beccles upbringing would have been reason enough for my interest in Nelson, but there were others. In course of time, I went to Caius College, Cambridge, where Nelson's father was at one time a junior Fellow. His portrait, by Sir William Beechey, hangs in the Hall, and I used to dine beneath it. Later still, when I began to delve into the admiral's history, I found that my own forbear, Joseph Warner FRS, an eye surgeon eminent in his day, had looked into Nelson's right eye, sightless from the wound he sustained in Corsica in 1794, and certified that 'the injury is fully equal to the loss of an eye'. This was in October 1797. Five months later, Nelson applied for expenses incurred as a result of the loss of his right arm in action at Teneriffe, and Joseph Warner was one of the eight examining surgeons who approved his claim. One of Joseph's ancestors was the first English settler in the West Indies, which were to become so familiar to Nelson, who would have seen his monument at St Kitts.

Finally, during the Second World War, I was appointed to the Secretariat of the Admiralty, and from the nature of my work, had access to the official Library, part of which was then housed in the archway over the Mall. On its shelves were the principal books on and about the admiral, and other material relevant to the study of his background. I did not miss the chance to use the resources at my disposal.

These are the reasons for my sustained interest in the character and career of a man who exercised the same fascination over his contemporaries that he has done over posterity. It is unlikely that much fresh material will come to light about him, but each succeeding biography will have its own particular emphasis. I have tried to assess how much Nelson was a man of his time.

OW

1
The
Rising
Man

HORATIO NELSON was an Englishman born in Norfolk in the middle of the eighteenth century. Each of these facts is important in considering his character and career. There is found a mixed strain of nationalities in many people of genius. With Nelson it was not so. There were no exotic marriages in his immediate ancestry, and his genius could only have developed as it did against a background of extended war. Had there been no War of American Independence, no long struggle with France between 1793 and 1815, Nelson would not have been remembered by posterity. He would have lived and died a capable sea officer, with a marked gift of friendship. Had his letters been preserved, those who read them would have remarked that his charm extended to the written word.

Nelson had a felicitous way of expression, clear, natural, rising sometimes to eloquence, which must always have given pleasure to his correspondents. This accounts for the fact that a substantial number of his missives were treasured long before the recipients had any idea that one day he would be famous. The extant letters, despatches and memoranda were collected into eight large volumes. Seven of them, edited by Sir Harris Nicolas, appeared during the 1840s. The eighth and last was published as recently as 1958. The documents necessarily form the basis of study. They are proof of Nelson's industry, if of nothing else. The fact that he died at the age of forty-seven, and that, almost certainly, a large number of letters and so on have disappeared or been destroyed, indicates that as a correspondent he was a prodigy.

He was also, to a marked degree, an autobiographer. He enjoyed writing accounts of events, mainly in letters to his family and friends, almost as much as acting in them: it was like having his cake and eating it. When he became a national figure, after the battle of the Nile in 1798, the editors of the *Naval Chronicle*, one of whom, John M'Arthur, afterwards had a hand in a ponderous official *Life*, asked him for a sketch of his career. This Nelson willingly supplied. The editors cooked it up in a style which ruined many of their biographical notices of leading naval characters, but Sir Harris Nicolas got hold of the original. This opened as follows:

Horatio Nelson, son of the Reverend Edmund Nelson, Rector of Burnham Thorpe, in the County of Norfolk, and Catherine his wife, daughter of Doctor Suckling, Prebendary of Westminster, whose [grand] mother was sister to Sir Robert Walpole, Earl of Orford.

I was born September 29th, 1758, in the Parsonage-house, was sent to the high-school at Norwich, and afterwards removed to North Walsham;

This wistful eight-year-old may be the young Nelson; opinions differ violently.

from whence, on the disturbance with Spain relative to Falkland's Islands, I went to sea with my uncle, Captain Maurice Suckling, in the *Raisonable* of 64 guns ...

All this was true, as far as it went, though Nelson actually went to a third school, at Downham Market, where he was remembered by another Norfolk stalwart, Captain George Manby, well known for a rocket apparatus he devised for saving life from shipwreck. The 'disturbance with Spain relative to Falkland's Islands' was a

13

ABOVE A young midshipman, thought by some to be
Nelson.
RIGHT The peaceful rectory at Burnham Thorpe where
Horatio was born, which remained his home during the
early years of his marriage.

matter in which Spain, France and Britain were all involved. It was settled, at least for some time to come, by the withdrawal of Spanish claims to the windswept group of islands in the South Atlantic, but, as an inconsiderable result, Nelson, at the age of twelve, began an apprenticeship which was to be of a varied kind.

The *Raisonable*'s French name (which, strictly speaking, should have been spelt with a second '*n*') derived from a prize taken during an earlier war. She was only three years old, and was to survive for nearly half a century. After Nelson had been seven months on her books, Captain Suckling arranged for him to go on a voyage to the West Indies aboard a merchantman. The vessel was the *Mary Ann*. Her owners were Messrs Hibbert, Purrier and Horton, and her master was John Rathbone.

Rathbone had once been in the Navy. He had served with Captain Suckling in HMS *Dreadnought* during the Seven Years War, in the course of which Suckling made his name. Rathbone may have been ready to oblige his old commander by taking one of his relations to sea with him, but it was with the men that Nelson worked. One and all, they loathed the Navy. The *Mary Ann* left London on 25 July 1771 for Jamaica. She also visited Tobago, and was back at home almost a year later.

If I did not improve my education [wrote Nelson], I returned a practical Seaman, with a horror of the Royal Navy and with a saying, then constant with the Seamen, '*Aft the most honour, forward the better man!*' It was many weeks before I got in the least reconciled to a Man-of-War; so deep was the prejudice rooted; and what pains were taken to instil this erroneous principle in a young mind!

Merchant seamen had every reason to detest the Navy, into which they were liable to be forced by the press gang, particularly in time of war. In the Navy, pay was poor, discipline harsh, the quarters crowded, the company miscellaneous – and there was no leave. The men did the work; the officers took the credit – that was the view drummed into young Nelson. In time, it was modified, but that first long voyage, in which he made acquaintance with the Caribbean, which he was soon to know well, was important. At least he had heard the point of view of seamen not in the King's service. From this fact, consequences flowed. Nelson understood men in a way he would never have done but for Suckling's initiative.

Maurice Suckling was a major factor in Nelson's life. Of excellent family, he had much influence, and he was a fighter. His great

moment had come in October 1757 when his ship, the *Dreadnought*, with two others, the *Augusta* and the *Edinburgh*, attacked a greatly superior number of Frenchmen, seven in all, including some heavy ships. The action took place near Cape François, in the West Indies, and the enemy were routed with heavy loss. Forrest, the senior captain, on seeing what he was up against, summoned his fellow commanders to a Council of War. This lasted less than a minute. Suckling and Langdon, the officers concerned, gave their views from the gangway, and all were of the same way of thinking – go for the enemy! They returned at once to their ships, and beat to quarters. Nelson heard the story from his uncle. He remembered it all his life.

A contemporary instrument. Navigation was one of the skills imparted to young officers during their early years at sea.

17

Suckling's next ship was the *Triumph* of 74 guns, and she was his last. The captain's final work would be ashore. The *Triumph* was a guard-ship at Chatham, and being on her books gave Nelson the chance to practise navigation in the estuaries of the Thames and Medway, where Drake was taught his trade. Nelson said he 'became a good pilot ... and confident of myself among rocks and sands, which has many times since been of the very greatest comfort to me'. He had reason to boast, for there are few areas of salt water with more hazards. Although it was a chilly life after the sun of the Caribbean, at least it was a bracing prelude to his next assignment, which was to the Arctic.

Once again, Nelson was lucky in those under whom he served. An expedition 'towards the North Pole', in the words of the time, was fitted out, in charge of Captain Lord Mulgrave, his pendant flying in the *Racehorse*. With Mulgrave went Captain Skeffington Lutwidge in the *Carcass*, Nelson being one of his midshipmen. Nelson was made coxswain of a cutter, and, he said, 'I prided myself in fancying I could navigate her better than any other boat in the ship.' As exploration, the venture was a failure, ice conditions forcing the ships to return in the later months of 1772. Almost at once, soon after he had reached the age of fifteen, Nelson was off to the East on board the frigate *Seahorse*.

The *Seahorse* was a veteran with battle honours to which she was destined to add. Built in 1748, she had been in the fleet which Sir Charles Saunders had taken up the St Lawrence in 1759, thus enabling Wolfe to win Quebec. Later in the same war, she had been with Admiral Cornish at the capture of Manila by the British, a fact which many historians find hard to credit, so firmly have the Philippines become associated with the United States. In 1772 her captain was George Farmer, and her Master's name was Surridge.

Farmer, who was killed in action within a few years, was what was known as a 'taut hand'. He believed in the lash, and used it often. The *Seahorse* was not a happy ship, and although Surridge was a first-class Master, and was much help in enlarging Nelson's education as a professional sea officer, neither Nelson nor Thomas Troubridge, his great friend of those early years, would dwell willingly on what they endured during this commission.

Winston Churchill once said that the naval traditions were rum, sodomy and the lash. Rum alleviated the horrors of the lash, and it may perhaps be useful to get the matter of punishment into some sort of perspective. In Nelson's day, in the armed forces, the Army no less than in the Navy, there were two very different worlds –

that of the 'People', as the men were called in ship's logs, and that of the officers. Even in a happy ship, the difference between them was great: in one such as the *Seahorse*, it was cruel. The men suffered, some of them over and over again, for the lash was no deterrent, and the word 'shell-back' had a connotation not always suspected. Among the commoner crimes were drunkenness, 'fighting' and 'insolence', which might mean anything.

A sadistic captain was not uncommon, and youngsters had to steel themselves to attend to the order 'hands to witness punishment' until they became as hardened to it as their nature allowed. Nelson himself took such punishments as part of the scheme of things, and the fact has also to be remembered that, like every boy of his time who was sent to school, he had been at the mercy of the birching pedagogue. 'Spare the rod and spoil the child' was then

Early evidence of the young Nelson's daring: his much cited encounter with a bear during the Arctic expedition of 1772–3.

21

The *Racehorse* and *Carcass* trapped in the ice which ruined the expedition, though not the fifteen-year-old Nelson's enjoyment. He had been made coxswain of one of the *Carcass*'s cutters and prided himself on his seamanship.

more than a catch-word; it was a rule of life. Some of Nelson's later actions will be better understood if this is borne in mind.

Nelson was in the *Seahorse* between the autumn of 1773 and December 1775, when he went down with fever at Bombay, and was ordered to go home. The Malabar and Coromandel coasts became known to him; so, to some extent, did the Persian Gulf and Ceylon. He thought Trincomalee the finest natural harbour he had seen, until, as a flag officer, he visited Milford Haven. And it was in Indian waters that he first saw guns fired in anger. Off Anjengo, on the Malabar coast, Captain Farmer intercepted an armed vessel in the service of Hyder Ali of Mysore. Hyder Ali and his son Tippoo were inveterate enemies of the British, although in February 1775, when the action took place, Britain was not officially at war with the Indian ruler. Farmer no doubt had his reasons for the action he took, which wasted much powder and shot to no ostensible purpose.

Nelson took passage home in the frigate *Dolphin*, Captain James Pigott, on 23 March 1776. He was lucky in his host and in the fact that, low as the climate had brought him, he did not die in the East, where mortality was high, although not as high as in the West Indies. The *Dolphin*, which was on her last commission, took six months over the journey. Like the *Seahorse*, she was a well-known ship. Built in 1751 at Woolwich, she was one of the first to be sheathed with copper, to keep her free from those marine growths which were so apt to slow down wooden hulls. She had taken Captain Samuel Wallis in 1767 to discover Tahiti.

Fever, and seeming lack of prospects, depressed Nelson, though he gradually recovered his spirits. 'A sudden glow of patriotism was kindled within me,' he would say later. He perceived a radiant orb, which seemed to beckon him on. He felt that it was intended to present 'my King and Country as my patron. My mind exulted in the idea. "Well, then," I exclaimed, "I will be a hero, and, confiding in Providence, I will brave every danger."'

It was a propitious time for such a resolve, for during the next few years the Navy would have need of as many 'heroes' as could be discovered. The War of American Independence had begun; indeed, when Nelson was on his way back to England, the Colonists declared their independence from the Mother Country.

In September 1776, Nelson was made acting lieutenant of the *Worcester*, a ship of the line. Her captain was Mark Robinson. By this time, Nelson's uncle Suckling had become Comptroller of the Navy, head of the Navy Board, which was concerned with ship

OPPOSITE 'The men who did the work' in ships of Nelson's time, from contemporary aquatints by Rowlandson. From the top corner: sailor, cabin boy, carpenter, cook.

construction and supplies, and thus very consequential. For this reason, and because Robinson seems to have liked Nelson for himself, his captain showed the young man special favour. The *Worcester* was engaged in convoy work to and from Gibraltar. Nelson said of this period, 'although my age might have been a sufficient cause for not entrusting me with charge of a Watch, yet Captain Robinson used to say: "he felt as easy when I was upon deck, as any Officer in the Ship."'

On 8 April 1777 Nelson passed his examination for lieutenant, and at once received his commission. Suckling was on the board of examiners, but did not mention his relationship until afterwards, so sure did he feel that his nephew would make a good impression. Nelson was appointed to the frigate *Lowestoffe*, Captain William Locker. Suckling would have had much to do with the choice of ship, and he chose well. It mattered nothing, then or at the time of a later promotion, that Nelson was under the regulation age for the rank, which was twenty. Such regulations were, at that time, more honoured in the breach than the observance.

The *Lowestoffe* had replaced a ship of the same name which had been at the taking of Quebec and at the relief of the city the following year. As for Locker, he was an ardent disciple of Lord Hawke. He had been in the fleet which had won the great chase victory of Quiberon Bay in 1759, and he had also served with the future Earl of St Vincent. He was the ideal man to rekindle the zeal which Suckling had implanted in Nelson years before. And, as his ship was destined for the West Indies, Nelson would be going to a highly important area – increasingly so when first France and then Spain gave armed support to the Americans.

From the point of view of trade, the West Indies were then the brightest jewel in the British crown. Jamaica and Barbados were the richest yielding possessions, but Britain held other islands, and so did the French, Spaniards, Dutch, Danes and Swedes. The whole area, had it not been for interloping stretching back in point of time to the sixteenth century, should have been Spanish, but in Nelson's day, the sharpest rivalry was between France and Britain. In any war between Britain and her North American colonists, control of the Caribbean would be of paramount importance. Nelson used to refer to the area as the Station of Honour. Unfortunately, it was also the station of disease, the wastage in human life from climatic conditions being many times that of battle. However, those who survived were apt to rise in their profession. This was Nelson's hope.

Captain William Locker, under whom Nelson served
as a lieutenant in the frigate *Lowestoffe*. Locker became
a lifelong friend, to whom Nelson wrote twenty years
later 'I have been your scholar; it is you who
taught me to board a Frenchman'.

Once at Jamaica, Locker allowed his young lieutenant the chance to 'cruise', that is, to reconnoitre, with the possibility of taking prizes. He gave him charge of a schooner, the *Little Lucy*, named after his daughter. 'In this vessel,' wrote Nelson, 'I made myself a complete pilot for all the passages through the . . . islands situated on the north side of Hispaniola.' Nelson's boast was that he grew confident among the cluster which includes Great and Little Inagua, and the Caicos and Turks Island groups. They lie to the north of the modern Haiti, which was then occupied by France. It was her western outpost in the area.

On 20 October 1777, Locker intercepted an American privateer, at a time when Nelson was on board the *Lowestoffe*, not the *Little Lucy*. The weather was bad, with a gale of wind and a high sea. The senior lieutenant was ordered to take a prize crew over to the privateer, but failed, owing to the severe conditions. Nelson related what followed. Locker called out: 'Have I no Officer in the Ship who can board the Prize?' The Master at once ran to the gangway. 'I stopped him,' said Nelson, saying 'It is my turn now, and if I come back, it is yours.' It is scarcely necessary to say that Nelson succeeded. He could not resist adding, in his account, 'this little incident has often occurred to my mind, and I know it is my disposition, that difficulties and dangers do but increase my desire of attempting them.'

The year following this incident, Admiral Sir Peter Parker arrived at Jamaica as Commander-in-Chief, and Nelson's prospects took an immediate upward turn. Parker and Maurice Suckling had been friends and comrades-in-arms, and Nelson was taken into the flag-ship *Bristol* in September 1778, as third lieutenant. He quickly rose to be first. In three months he had further promotion. He was made a Commander and given charge of the brig *Badger*, in which he was sent to the bay of Honduras to protect the settlers. He was in the ship less than a year, being succeeded by his life-long friend, Cuthbert Collingwood. Parker, who could spot talent better than most men, made Nelson a post captain in June 1779, when he was not quite twenty-one. He was given command of the sloop *Hinchinbrooke*, recently taken from the French and re-named. As the appointment was in due course confirmed by the Admiralty, Nelson was 'made', in the phrase of the time. No one could overtake him on the captain's list, and he had only to live long enough when, by the strict rule of seniority which then prevailed, he would get his flag.

Parker never did better work for his country than when favouring Nelson and Collingwood, so different, and yet so complementary to one another. In their turn, they never forgot his kindness, which Collingwood was one day able to repay by promoting Parker's grandson. Collingwood, a Northumbrian, was almost exactly ten years older than Nelson, and had endured three difficult years as a lieutenant under a contemptible commander. Despite the great difference in age (more apparent then than it would ever be again), the two men were already close to one another; and of jealousy, on the part of Collingwood, that Nelson had become senior to him, there was never a trace.

At this time, Jamaica was in serious danger of invasion from Hispaniola, for the French admiral d'Estaing had arrived there from Martinique with a fleet and an army. Writing to Locker, who had by then gone home, Nelson said – 'Jamaica is turned upside down since you left it.' He himself lived ashore at Port Royal during the crisis, where he was in charge of the batteries.

The alarm passed, and Parker then decided to take the initiative against the Spaniards in Nicaragua. It was a misguided notion. The season was wrong, the expedition ill-equipped; and, although Nelson enjoyed campaigning ashore, there was not much glory to be won in Central America. But he was the right age for adventure, and his description, written many years afterwards, suggests that he remembered its glow.

I quitted my ship, carried troops in boats one hundred miles up a river which none but Spaniards since the time of the buccaneers had ever ascended ... I boarded (if I may be allowed the expression), an outpost of the Enemy, situated on an Island in the river ... made batteries, and afterwards fought them, and was a principal cause of our success.

The success was very limited. It consisted of the capture of Fort St Juan, on the river of that name, though even that took place just after Nelson himself had returned to the coast. A sketch he made of the scene shows the Spanish flag, which at that time featured the cross of Burgundy, still flying over the principal buildings.

Collingwood was explicit in stating the object of the foray.

It was proposed by the River St. Juan, and the Lakes Nicaragua and Leon, to pass by a navigation of boats into the South Sea [the Pacific]. The plan was formed without a sufficient knowledge of the country, which presented difficulties that were not to be surmounted by human skill or perseverance. The river was difficult to proceed on from the rapidity of the current, and the several falls over the rocks, which intercepted the navigation, and the climate was deadly; no constitution could resist its effects.

Both Nelson and Collingwood were tough enough to survive, although with Nelson it was touch and go. Collingwood's ship's company was almost obliterated: he recorded that he buried 180 out of 200 men. These, he said, fell 'not by the hand of the enemy, but sunk under the contagion of the climate'.

The 'contagion' affected Nelson so badly that he had to invalid at Port Royal, and he asked leave to go home to recover. Before he left the West Indies, he was appointed to the frigate *Janus*, though he never took her to sea. He was too ill. Instead, after a spell in the home of Lady Parker, he became the guest of Captain the Honourable William Cornwallis, in the *Lion*, ship of the line. Nelson said that Cornwallis's 'care and attention saved my life'. The two men became friends, and Cornwallis was certainly among the most important contacts Nelson had had until then.

Cornwallis, a younger brother of a general who was shortly to be forced to capitulate with his army at Yorktown in Virginia, owing to a failure in British sea-power, was a post captain of fifteen years standing. When still in his early teens, he had been present at the taking of Louisbourg, and was thus one of the many who imbued Nelson with emulation of the spirit which had prevailed during the Seven Years War (1756-62) and the conquest of Canada. Like Suckling and Locker, Cornwallis was full of the fighting spirit, and like them an admirer of Hawke, under whom he had served at Quiberon. Nelson was to hear of him later on in the war as one of Rodney's captains, and much later still as the admiral commanding Britain's principal fleet. Cornwallis would have had much to impart to Nelson as the *Lion* made her way home. Nelson would convalesce at Bath fortified by knowledge of some of the best men in the Navy. Suckling was no longer among them, for he had died when Nelson was still a lieutenant in the *Bristol*.

Nelson was an invalid for some months. He wrote at the end of January 1791 to Locker that although he had not quite recovered full use of his limbs, his 'inside was a new man'. His family, especially his father, loved Bath, the climate being so much milder than that of Burnham Thorpe. Nelson was at last able to get to know his brothers and sisters well. His mother had died when he was nine. His brother Maurice, five years his senior, was a favourite with Horatio. Maurice had a post in the Navy Office (again thanks to Suckling) and would be a useful source of professional news. William, an uncouth creature, next to Horatio in age and a year

View of PORT ROYAL and KINGSTON HARBOUR in the Island of JAMAICA.

older, was a parson, though not a spiritually minded one. Two sisters, Susanna, who was older, and Catherine, who was younger, came to mean something in their brother's life.

Nelson, who was the best of sons, and affectionate to all his kindred, had some prize money put by. He spent it freely, as was always his way, for he was no saver. He must have appeared extraordinarily frail at this time, as well as being small and slight. He was only five feet four inches high, if a mark in the old Admiralty Board Room known as 'Nelson's spot' is a true guide, but he was well proportioned. By nature he was sociable and gay, and even ill-health did not make him morose.

By August 1781 Nelson was sufficiently recovered to ask the Admiralty for a new ship. Seeing that the war was at its height, and going badly, there was no difficulty in obliging him. He was given the *Albemarle*, which was rated as a frigate. Like the *Hinchinbrook*, she was a prize, taken earlier the same year. She had been re-named

Here, Nelson lived ashore in charge of the batteries at a time when there was danger of a French attack.

31

A view of Bath's North
Parade in 1773. Nelson was
to return here often to
recuperate after his voyages.

after that doughty warrior, George Monck, Duke of Albemarle, who had fought the Dutch during the previous century. Monck used to say that 'valour and sufferance' were the principal qualities necessary in those who took up arms for their country. Nelson was eager to show valour, but 'sufferance' was his lot. He had command of his new ship for two years, and saw out the rest of the war in her, but there was no glory to be won on the missions he was assigned.

It would almost be supposed, to try my constitution [he wrote]. I was kept the whole winter in the North Sea. In April 1782, I sailed with a convoy for Newfoundland and Quebec, under the orders of Captain Thomas Pringle. From Quebec, during a cruise off Boston, I was chased by three French ships of the Line, and the *Iris* frigate; as they all beat me in sailing very much, I had no chance left, but running them amongst the shoals of St. George's Bank. This alarmed the Line of Battle Ships, and they quitted the pursuit; but the Frigate continued, and at sunset was little more than gun shot distant, when the Line of Battleships being out of sight, I ordered the main topsail to be laid to the mast, when the Frigate tacked, and rejoined her consorts.

In his autobiographical fragment, Nelson harped on his seamanship as much as on his personal courage, which was odd, since no one doubted either. But in his account of his time in the *Albermarle*, he omitted one episode completely. In March 1783, towards the very end of the war, he got together some ships, and at least one captain who was very reluctant, to attack the French-held Turks Island, north of Hispaniola, and in an area of sea that Nelson purported to know well. The enemy were thoroughly prepared, and he was repulsed. In the way habitual to him, he blamed himself, and gave credit to those under his orders.

A few months earlier, at New York, he had been attached for a time to a fleet commanded by Lord Hood. This was the one which had been victorious under Rodney at the battle of April 1782 off Dominica which had saved Jamaica from invasion, and in which de Grasse, the French Commander-in-Chief, had been captured, together with his flag-ship. As Rodney's second, Hood had played a notable part on the great day, and had won himself a peerage. Nelson was eager to be accepted as being of Hood's circle, and there is evidence that Hood thought highly of him. The admiral had among his officers Prince William Henry, the third son of George III and one day to reign as William IV. The Prince later recalled Nelson as being:

... the merest boy of a captain I ever beheld; and his dress was worthy of attention. He had on a full laced uniform; his lank unpowdered hair

was tied in a stiff Hessian tail of an extraordinary length; the old-fashioned flaps of his waistcoat added to the general quaintness of his figure . . . I had never seen anything like it before . . . My doubts were, however, removed when Lord Hood introduced me to him. There was something irresistibly pleasing in his address and conversation, and an enthusiasm, when speaking on professional subjects, that showed he was no common being.

Hood recommended the Prince to Nelson as one who had made a close study of tactics. The Prince, who had a keener eye for *minutiae* than for larger matters, never revised his opinion about Nelson's qualities. At the end of a wearing struggle, when most captains were jaded, Nelson was not. He attended the Prince on a visit to Spanish-held Havana, a courtesy made possible once peace was certain, and then sailed for home.

OPPOSITE Prince William Henry, later William IV, as a midshipman. He met Nelson when they were both young officers, and took an immediate liking to him.

2
West-Indian
Waters

ONE OF THE DIFFERENCES between the warfare of the early eighteenth century and of later eras was the speed at which Englishmen hastened to make, or renew, acquaintance with their late enemies, once peace was on the way. The bitterness which came in with the French Revolution was absent. Even before the Treaty of Versailles, involving the warring countries, was formally ratified, Nelson was planning a jaunt to France.

This did not last long – only from November 1783 to January 1784. He did not get far, just to St Omer, south-east of Calais, and he did not admire what he saw. But he took pains to try to learn some French, and after a time he came to understand it tolerably well, though he did not attempt to speak it if he could help it. He met one or two sea officers, including a certain Captain Alexander Ball, whom he thought a bit of a coxcomb because he wore the latest pattern of naval uniform. That, as Prince William Henry had noted, was not Nelson's style at all. He also fell in love, and for the second time. When on a visit to Canada in the *Albemarle* he had fancied a local beauty, but was dissuaded from paying his attentions on the advice of Alexander Davison, who became his friend and prize agent. In France, it was a certain Miss Andrews. He took the matter seriously enough this time to write to an uncle, William Suckling, asking if he would supplement his half pay if he took the plunge. He also befriended the lady's brother, who was in the Navy.

It all came to nothing, however, and in March 1784, when in London, Nelson called on Lord Howe, who was then presiding at the Admiralty. He was given a ship. She was the *Boreas*, a frigate built at Hull. The appointment was somewhat surprising, for in time of peace commands were scarce, and Nelson aspired to Hood's circle, not to Howe's. There is no doubt who was the greater of the two. Howe had held, with distinction, every post open to a sea officer.

Nelson's one and only peacetime commission in command of a ship was in many ways frustrating. He set sail for the West Indies in May, the *Boreas* cluttered up with what he called 'lumber'. There were a number of young gentlemen, candidates for the quarter-deck, whom Nelson had taken with him to oblige their friends. There was his brother William, who thought he would try a spell as a naval chaplain; above all, there was Lady Hughes. She was a special trial, for not only did she require special accommodation, but she was, in Nelson's phrase, an 'eternal clack'. He had to be particularly attentive to her because she was the wife of Rear

PREVIOUS PAGES The frigate *Boreas* off the island of Nevis. Nelson commanded her from 1784 to 1787, years spent attempting to curb the illicit trade between the West Indies and the rebellious American colonies.

Admiral Sir Richard Hughes, baronet, who was Nelson's Commander-in-Chief.

The Leeward Island Station, for which Nelson was bound, presented a scene of some intricacy. Nelson put the matter succinctly in the account which he gave of his three years in the area.

This Station opened a new scene to the Officers of the British Navy. The Americans, when Colonists, possessed almost all the trade from America to our West India Islands: and on the return to Peace, they forgot, on this occasion, they became foreigners, and of course had no right to trade in the British Colonies. Our Governors and Custom-house Officers pretended, that by the Navigation Act they had a right to trade; and all the West Indians wished what was so much for their interest.

Having given Governors, Custom-house Officers and Americans notice of what I would do, I seized many of their Vessels, which brought all parties upon me; and I was so persecuted from one Island to another, that I could not leave my Ship. But conscious rectitude bore me through it; and I was supported, when the business came to be understood, from home; and I proved . . . that a Captain of a Man of War is in duty bound to support all the Maritime Laws, by his Admiralty commission alone, without becoming a Custom-house Officer.

Rear Admiral Hughes, who to Nelson's mind 'bowed and scraped too much', gave his captains no support, rather the reverse. His idea was to wink the eye, and to keep in with the Governors. However, in the autumn of 1784, who should arrive on the Station but Cuthbert Collingwood in the frigate *Mediator*. Here was someone after Nelson's heart, eager to follow his example in measures to suppress illicit trade. Collingwood's younger brother Wilfred later joined the squadron in the sloop *Rattler*, and Americans got short shrift from any of them. Wilfred actually wore himself out in the service, and died at sea.

The policing work was unpopular, the tedium almost unendurable. Barbados, Antigua, Montserrat, Nevis, St Kitts, that was the usual round. Rarely, as in November 1784, Hughes gave orders for work which offered some scope for initiative. Nelson was sent to survey the harbour of St Johns, in the Virgin Islands, which was well to the west of his usual beat.

There were, however, alleviations. Nelson and Collingwood enjoyed hospitality at the house of Captain Moutray, who was the Commissioner for the Navy Office at Antigua. Mrs Moutray was a woman of charm and understanding. The bachelor captains admired her, and Nelson took a fancy to her boy, who later went to sea and died on active service in the Mediterranean. In the

Moutray's house at English Harbour, Nelson and Collingwood drew portraits of one another, the general cordiality being undisturbed by another act of officiousness on Nelson's part. On one occasion he questioned Moutray's right to fly a broad pendant from a ship in the harbour, in the belief that Moutray's was a civil appointment, not a naval one.

While in the West Indies, Nelson did not lack for old acquaintances. Cuthbert Collingwood had no sooner been ordered back to England than Prince William Henry joined him in the frigate *Pegasus*, of which he had been given command. The arrival presented problems, for in July 1786 Hughes went home, and Nelson was left senior officer on the station, responsible for looking after the Prince.

He was a handful. Twenty-one years of age, with the distinction of having been in action under Rodney in Spanish waters, he was very conscious of his position, and a martinet. The Admiralty had appointed an experienced lieutenant, Isaac Schomberg, in the hope that he would guide the Prince aright. The result was disastrous. Schomberg fell foul of him, and was soon under close arrest.

Nelson spent many happy hours ashore at the Moutray's home in English Harbour, Antigua (*above*), where his friend Collingwood made this portrait of him (*left*).

41

Occupied as he was with Royalty, Nelson was also courting a
widow. She was Frances Nisbet, niece of the President of Nevis,
and she had a boy of five, Josiah. Nelson loved children, and he
was soon Josiah's slave. Prince William Henry did nothing to
discourage the match, and on 11 March 1787 Nelson and Fanny
were married at St Kitts, with the Prince as best man.

Nelson was by then preparing for home.

Happy shall I be when that time arrives [he wrote to Locker]. No man
has had more illness or trouble on a Station than I have experienced; but
let me lay a balance on the other side – I am married to an amiable woman,
that far makes amends for everything; indeed, until I married her, I never
knew happiness. And I am morally certain she will continue to make me
a happy man for the rest of my days.

42

A portrait of Lady Nelson
painted some time after their marriage.

44

The sentiment was elevated, but the language was scarcely that of passion.

The *Boreas* reached Portsmouth in July 1787 but she was not paid off at once. She was sent round to the Medway, and her people were aboard until 30 November. Recent research has shown that one of them, a cooper called James Carse, immediately got into very serious trouble, about which Nelson was called to give evidence.

When in Antigua, Carse seems to have been affected by the sun, or so Nelson thought, and he became solitary and melancholy. Very soon after he was discharged, he murdered a woman called Sarah Hayes at a house in Shadwell – an apparently motiveless crime. Carse was apprehended, and he was defended at the Old Bailey by an able Counsel, William Garrow, who called Nelson as a character witness. Nelson showed considerable knowledge of Carse, and thus by implication of the rest of his men, and he described in evidence how he himself had been affected by the sun. 'I have been out of my senses,' he said; 'it hurts the brain.' Nelson felt confident that Carse's action was not premeditated. 'I should as soon suspect myself,' he said, 'because I am hasty, he is not.'

With what may seem remarkable humanity for those days, Carse was recommended for clemency and received it, though he was confined. In 1789 the First Lord of the Admiralty, Chatham, wrote to Nelson about a pardon, and to enquire whether Nelson would be willing to take Carse to sea with him again. Nelson's answer is not on record, and neither is Carse's ultimate fate. In any case, Nelson was without a ship from December 1787 until January 1793.

What this fact cost in frustration, to an ambitious man not yet thirty years old, and at the height of his always considerable energies, would be hard to estimate. It was not as if nothing was astir in the scene abroad, especially in France, where the Revolution was about to erupt. There was also trouble in Spain, over rights in the North Pacific, and a fleet was mobilized as a precaution. Many officers got appointments, including Collingwood. Not so Nelson. 'I made use of every interest to get a Ship, aye, even a boat to serve my Country,' he wrote, 'but in vain: there was a prejudice at the Admiralty evidently against me, which I can neither guess at, or in the least account for.'

At the Rector's wish, Horatio and Fanny lived mainly at the Parsonage House at Burnham Thorpe, though they visited relations elsewhere, and sometimes made excursions to London. Fanny and her father-in-law were always in accord. As for Nelson, it was his

The Honourable William Cornwallis, with whom Nelson sailed home in the *Lion*. He was a member of the professional dining-clubs which gave Nelson a welcome chance to meet his fellow officers in the frustrating years ashore without a command.

way to become absorbed in whatever he was doing, and this now included farming. He was poor, but even so, his condition was far removed from that of the Norfolk labourers around him. Nelson tried to interest Prince William Henry in their wretched plight, on yearly earnings of £23. The Prince was a faithful correspondent, but the condition of the rural poor would not have been a matter of concern to one who advocated the continuance of the Slave Trade, and one who, writing to Nelson from the *Pegasus* reported: 'In my own ship I go on pretty well. . . . I have had two Courts Marshal, one on the Master at Arms who was broke and received 100 lashes. . . .'

Nelson was fond of coursing. He was also a great reader, with the touching belief that if anyone published a book, they must have something to say. The cadences of the King James Bible had

46

been familiar to him from his earliest years, and he was a Shake-spearian. Half-remembered quotations from the plays occur in his letters, and there are references to Swift and Addison. Samuel Johnson, who died the year Nelson commissioned the *Boreas*, once told a young poet to 'give nights and days to the study of Addison if you mean to be a good writer or, what is more worth, an honest man'. Neither Nelson nor Collingwood had any need of this advice, and both men also enjoyed travels. Dampier's *Voyages* was among Nelson's favourite reading.

He was popular with his fellow captains. In Pepys's time, senior officers who had served with Prince Rupert at sea had formed a dining club, which had been in existence on and off ever since. During the eighteenth century it became regularized under the title of 'Royal Naval Club of 1765'. Nelson belonged to this club, and to another, the 'Navy Club of 1785', of which Sir Peter Parker was the first President. Many of the leading officers, including Cornwallis, Sir John Jervis, later Earl of St Vincent, and Adam Duncan joined one or both. Nelson attended two dinners in 1788 and one during the following year. He would not have omitted any chance of listening to the professional talk of equals in the Navy. And at last, when Britain was on the eve of one of the most pro-tracted wars in her history, his luck changed. 'On the 30th of January,' he recorded, 'I was commissioned in the very hand-somest way for the *Agamemnon*, 64 [guns], and was put under the command of that great man and excellent officer, Lord Hood, appointed to the command in the Mediterranean.'

3 HMS

Agamemnon

NELSON SELDOM made use of Latin tags, but he did so when giving Fanny news of his re-employment. '*Post nubila Phoebus*' – after clouds, sunshine: that was what he felt. It was an attitude unlikely to be shared by his wife, who would be losing a loved companion, perhaps for years.

> The Admiralty so smile upon me [wrote Nelson], that really I am as much surprised as when they frowned. Lord Chatham [First Lord at the time] made many apologies for not having given me a ship before this time, and said, that if I chose to take a Sixty-four to begin with, I should be appointed to one as soon as she was ready; and whenever it was in his power, I should be removed into a Seventy-four. Everything indicates war.

The *Agamemnon*, Nelson's first ship-of-the-line command, was a vessel for which he soon formed a tremendous attachment. She had been built by Henry Adams at Buckler's Hard on the Beaulieu River, and had been launched in 1774. As a new ship, she had fired her guns at Rodney's victory off Dominica. She sailed well, and in Nelson's eyes was the finest ship afloat. He was happy to be serving with Hood rather than with Howe, who had command in the Channel. He took Josiah with him to sea, together with several other Norfolk lads. The most notable was William Hoste, a parson's son, brightest of his immediate pupils.

War with France was not far away, and Nelson welcomed the prospect. The fiercer the war, the better the chance of advancement and adventure, and he longed for both.

As so often before and since, the general idea was that the trouble would 'soon be over'. The undisciplined, atheistic Revolutionaries would never create stable conditions, and the Crown of France would be restored. Spain, Austria and other Continental powers were Britain's allies. Howe's fleet would watch the one at Brest. Hood would blockade Toulon, ensuring the safe flow of trade to the Levant. It worked out differently.

France declared war on Britain in February 1793, occupied the Austrian Netherlands, which was in itself a major blow to British trade, and soon showed herself able to reorganize armies, even fleets, with speed. But she was not yet united, and a Royalist element at Toulon allowed Hood's ships, and those of Spain, to enter the harbour. Had sufficient troops been available, the area might have been held, but there were not enough men for the purpose. One of Nelson's first missions, when he reached the Mediterranean, was to Naples, a friendly Court with a close

PREVIOUS PAGES '*Building of HMS Agamemnon 64 guns, at Bucklers Hard 1780. H. Adams Master Shipwright.*'

OPPOSITE Sir William Hamilton, British Minister at Naples, first met Nelson in 1793 – the beginning of a friendship that was to last till the end of Hamilton's life.

50

connection with Spain. He reached there in September 1793, his business being to ensure the despatch of troops to help the alliance.

This was Nelson's earliest acquaintance with a place with which his name would be associated, though not with advantage. King Ferdinand was affability itself. So was his chief Minister, Sir John Acton, an expatriate who had inherited an English baronetcy. As for Sir William Hamilton, the British Minister, he had been in Naples almost thirty years, the last few of them as the husband of a well-known beauty, Emma Hart, who had once been the mistress of his nephew, Charles Greville. In his youth, Hamilton had served in the Guards, and been a friend of Nelson's hero, James Wolfe. Although over sixty, he was still vigorous, and active in getting Nelson what he wanted. Nelson was only a few days at Naples, but he took Josiah ashore with him. He wrote home to Fanny: 'Lady Hamilton has been wonderfully kind and good to Josiah. She is a young woman of amiable manners and who does honour to the station to which she is raised.'

Emma Hamilton, although often savagely caricatured in later life, caught the imagination of many. Here she is as seen by three artists: (*left to right*) Romney, Angelica Kauffman and Lawrence.

53

English residents evacuate Toulon. The withdrawal of the English fleet from Toulon, which Hood lost to the French revolutionary forces in 1793, strengthening considerably the position of French naval power in the Mediterranean.

Although Ferdinand sent troops to Hood, they proved useless, and they committed atrocities on prisoners, as Josiah noted. The Spaniards were little help, and touchy to the last degree. Indeed, they were soon to defect from the alliance. Besiegers pressed the perimeter ever more closely, helped by skilful siting of batteries by a young officer of artillery, Napoleon Bonaparte. Before the end of the year, the port had become untenable. That, perhaps, was inevitable, but what was culpable was the admiral's failure to destroy the French fleet when he had the chance to do so completely.

Both Collingwood – who was then with Howe in the Channel – and Nelson, who said 'one hour will burn the French fleet', felt the failure keenly, although Nelson would never ascribe any blame to Hood, for whom he had an admiration, not shared by all his contemporaries. Hood left the operation in the hands of Captain Sir Sidney Smith, who happened to be in the area as a volunteer, and who, with ineffable assurance, convinced Hood that he was the

man for the job. But when Hood left, with his ships packed with refugees, the beaches running with blood as the Revolutionaries slaughtered their compatriots, the work was half done. 'Great talkers do the least, we see,' said Nelson bitterly. The French put such energy into building and repair that soon the country had a formidable southern-based naval armament once more, 'a fleet in being', which would need constant watching.

In October 1793, a month significant for Nelson, who recalled Locker's engagement which had ended so creditably, Nelson, cruising off the east coast of Sardinia, encountered a squadron of five French ships, including three frigates, one of them *La Melpomène* of 44 guns, a powerful vessel. Nelson had only 345 men at quarters, others having been landed to serve ashore, but he did not hesitate to attack. He engaged the enemy for four hours, had one man killed and six wounded, and only broke off after making sure that he had the full concurrence of his officers. Afterwards he wrote a passage in his Journal of much significance, expressing as it did that trust in Providence which he had learnt from his father.

When I lay me down to sleep I recommend myself to the care of Almighty God, when I awake I give myself up to His direction, amidst all the evils that threaten me, I will look up to Him for help and question not that He will either avert them or turn them to my advantage though I know neither the time nor the manner of my death, I am not at all solicitous about it because I am sure that He knows them both, and that He will not fail to support and comfort me.

Once Toulon had been lost as a base, there remained as possibilities Minorca, with its fine harbour at Port Mahon, and Corsica. The larger island had recently been ceded to France by the Genoese, but their rule was unpopular, and many efforts had been made in the past to seek British protection. Hood and General Paoli, the Corsican patriot, well known to Johnson and Boswell, made contact, and Hood decided to mount an operation to expel the French garrisons.

This meant an amphibious campaign in which the main work would fall to the Navy. Nelson, who had enjoyed fighting ashore in Nicaragua, had a low opinion of the soldiers with whom he was asked to co-operate, but on his own men he could depend. They did splendid work ashore, hauling guns up mountain sides, and giving an example of energy to all concerned. The campaign lasted for over seven months, and resistance was stubborn. Bastia, in the north-east, surrendered in May 1794, and Calvi, in the north-west, some weeks later. A Viceroy, Gilbert Elliot, later Earl of Minto, was installed, and he never had the smallest doubt that it was Nelson's exertions which had been a principal factor in the success.

It was won at cost. The 'Agamemnons', as Nelson called his men, suffered heavily, mainly from sickness, and Nelson himself did not escape. One of his closest subordinates was a frigate captain, Thomas Fremantle, extracts from whose Diary have been printed only within the last few years. He was constantly with Nelson, whose activity surpassed his own, which was considerable. Fremantle, not Nelson, reported that they both had narrow escapes near Bastia on 19 April 1794, when a shot knocked Nelson down. Next time it was very serious for Nelson.

It was when the assault on Calvi was at its height that he received a wound resulting in the loss of sight to his right eye, though not the eye itself. In his Journal under the date of 12 July 1794, Nelson wrote: 'The enemy opened a heavy fire at daylight from the town ... seldom (very extraordinary) missing our battery. At

56

7 o'clock C[aptain] N[elson] was much bruized in the face and eyes by sand from the works struck by shot.' He wrote to Hood the same day, saying 'I got a little hurt this morning: not much, as you may judge from my writing.' He spared Fanny the news at first, for he continued his letters regularly and most affectionately, but to William Suckling he wrote more fully.

My right eye is entirely cut down; but the Surgeons flatter me I shall not entirely lose the sight of that eye. At present I can distinguish light from dark, but no object: it confined me one day, when, thank God, I was enabled to attend to my duty. I feel the want of it, but, such is the chance of War, it was within a hair's breadth of taking off my head.

It was the following January before he told Fanny: 'My eye is grown worse, and is in almost total darkness, and very painful at times; but never mind, I can see very well with the other.'

The origin of the persisting legend that Nelson wore a patch over his bad eye arose from the fact that he had a shade made, attached to his uniform hat, to protect the *good* one from glare. Afflicting as the wound was, and often troublesome, within a few weeks he appeared just the same. Of the many artists who later attempted his portrait, the majority distinguished no difference between the two eyes. This was so even in the case of a Leghorn miniaturist, who worked on Nelson within six months of the wound. There were different views about this representation. 'Josiah,' Nelson told Fanny, 'says the picture is not the least like me. Everybody else says it is, but I believe he is right.' Certainly a very different result appeared from the first documented portrait, completed by John Francis Rigaud in 1781.

By the winter of 1794, the *Agamemnon* and her ship's company were much the worse for wear and war. Lord Hood had sailed for home in the *Victory* in October, and under the regime of his successor, William Hotham, a good deal of laxity was allowed. One hundred and fifty of Nelson's men were in hospital, of whom only a hundred recovered, and Nelson himself, together with Fremantle and others, lived ashore at the Tuscan port of Leghorn while the ship was slowly refitting.

On Fremantle's evidence – and he was no laggard lover himself – Nelson took up with what was known as a 'dolly'. She spoke French, and there survives a solitary note from Nelson to her, written in that language, indicating that her name was Adelaide Correglia. On 3 December, Fremantle dined with the pair, afterwards going to the opera, where John Udney, the British Consul,

OVERLEAF Ships in which Nelson served: *Agamemnon, Vanguard, Elephant* and *Victory*.

57

introduced him to a 'very handsome Greek girl'. Udney understood the needs of wartime sailors.

On Nelson's part, it was quite an attachment, though his letters
to his wife continued to be as affectionate as ever. Nelson was
incapable of being half-hearted in anything, and on Fremantle's
showing, the affair lasted a good many months, for Adelaide
actually dined on board the *Agamemnon* the following summer.
Fremantle added that it was a 'very bad dinner'. He had already
noted that Nelson 'makes himself ridiculous with that woman'.
What Josiah thought of it all is impossible to say, but the way of
life of captains of HM ships was not one into which midshipmen
were wont to enquire. They had their own sorts of relaxation, as
did the men when in port. Some of Nelson's hospital cases were
venereal.

Hood's successor, Hotham, was no sort of man for Nelson. He
allowed his officers, among whom discipline was lax, to 'frolic' at
Leghorn, and twice, in the year 1795, he allowed a chance of a
decisive success to evade him. The first time was on 13 March, off
Genoa, when there seemed a chance of a full-scale fleet action. The
Ça Ira, one of the large French ships concerned, became dismasted.
Her escape was gallantly delayed by Fremantle in his frigate, the
Inconstant, which received a broadside. Nelson came up to his
support, but the *Ça Ira* escaped for that day. On the 14th, this ship,
and the *Censeur*, which was towing her, was cut off and surrendered, credit being shared between Fremantle and Nelson. Although Nelson and the second in command, Admiral Goodall,
urged Hotham to pursue the French with his undamaged ships,
Hotham spoke words which to Nelson were like wounds. 'We have
done very well. We must be contented.' It was just such a sentence,
spoken by Rodney, which had so grieved Hood in the hour of
success at the battle off Dominica in 1782. Nelson knew that the
true measure of an admiral was the way in which he followed up an
advantage.

The *Agamemnon*, considering the vigour of her attack, escaped
lightly, with only seven men wounded. Fremantle had three killed
and fourteen wounded. 'Providence certainly protects me and all
who sail with me,' wrote Nelson to Fanny, but, he added 'Goodall
and myself think we have done nothing in comparison to what we
might, would the Admiral have pursued our victory ... but we
want Lord Hood to command us – we should have had a glorious
victory!' It was some weeks before Nelson and Fremantle had the
chance to talk the action over. Fremantle noted: 'Nelson made me

many *compliments*. I know why!' There were too few captains with their zeal on the station.

In July, when Nelson was on detached service with three frigates and a cutter, he fell in with the French fleet and was chased back to S. Fiorenzo, the Corsican anchorage used by Hotham. A week later, Hotham sighted the French at sea and ordered a general chase, but the enemy escaped with only the loss of one of their rear ships, the *Alcide*, which blew up before Hotham could take possession. Almost worn out as she was, the *Agamemnon* managed to be in the lead, but Nelson was disappointed by a shift of wind in engaging the opponent he had chosen. As before, he felt that Hotham's chase was not conducted in the spirit of a Hawke or a Hood.

One official mark of distinction did come to Nelson in Hotham's time. He was made a Colonel of Marines. At that period there were four such appointments which, though honorary, carried the pay of the rank in addition to that of captain in the Navy. The Colonelcies were given to those high on the captain's list, but lapsed when the holders reached flag rank.

The honour was appropriate in Nelson's case, so often had he served in military operations. He was next ordered by Hotham to co-operate with the Austrian army, which was vainly attempting to stem the triumphant progress of the French in Italy. For a year and more, Nelson would be engaged in attacking enemy supply ships, since no opportunity arose of a further fleet action, and in withdrawing naval stores from strategic places, including Corsica. It was becoming clear to those at home that, for a time at least, it would not be possible to retain a strong fleet in the Mediterranean, so badly were matters going. 'The French fight on shore like our seamen,' Nelson wrote to Fanny, 'they never stop, and know not the word *halt*.'

It was a sad stage in Nelson's career, and he could have been forgiven had he felt despondent and war-weary. This, however, would have been unlike him. 'How I hate pessimists!' exclaimed Lord Fisher a century later. 'Shoot them at sight in war!' Nelson felt the same. England was indeed often in his mind, but his outlook improved with the advent of Sir John Jervis, who replaced Hotham as Commander-in-Chief. Here was a man to whom he could look up, and with better reason than with Hood. Jervis had been with Saunders and Wolfe at Quebec. His whole career had been that of a fighting seaman. His promotions had been through service not interest. The standard of his discipline was a by-word, and he

recognized zeal in subordinates. Jervis took to Nelson at once, gave him an independent inshore command, authorized him to fly a broad pendant as a commodore, and encouraged him in every way.

In June 1796, Nelson shifted his pendant from the *Agamemnon* to the *Captain* of 74 guns. It was a sad parting, and only Nelson could have protracted it so long, for the *Agamemnon* was worn out. She would need a skilful refit at home before she was good for further service. In her existing state, she would be lucky if she got back to England without mishap.

OPPOSITE Illness and the wild coastline of Corsica took their toll on Nelson's men during the seven-month campaign against the French.

4 Fame

"VICTORY"

WOUNDED · AT · TENERIFFE ··
JULY · 24 · 1797 ··

THE YEAR 1796 was one of alarm. There were many critical phases during the long war with France. Often they were due to the subversion, defeat or exhaustion of Continental allies, but in 1796 matters were made worse by the laxity with which Hood's brother, Lord Bridport, conducted the watch on the French Atlantic ports. It was of particular consequence because Ireland was in a state of turmoil; Wolfe Tone, the leading spirit of an organization called the United Irishmen, had invited help from France; and with Spain now an enemy, Bonaparte at large in Italy, and a Dutch fleet at French disposal, the United Kingdom seemed highly vulnerable.

Jervis had to base his ships on Lisbon and Gibraltar, but Gibraltar, as so often in the past, was under threat from Spain, and it was on Portugal that he relied for a secure anchorage. He did not relinquish his hold on the Mediterranean in any defeatist spirit, being determined to return there in strength whenever possible. But it seemed that this event might be delayed some time, for in July the French entered Leghorn, and at once began to encourage a revolt against British rule in Corsica. As the island was dependent on Italy for foodstuffs, its future value to Britain became doubtful. Nelson was sent to seize the island of Elba as an alternative advanced base, one from which Leghorn could be blockaded. Meanwhile, there was much to do in withdrawing the Corsican garrisons.

The work occupied Nelson for part of the autumn and winter season, and at the beginning of December he went to Gibraltar, where Jervis ordered him to shift his broad pendant from the *Captain* to the frigate *Minerva*, a vessel taken from the French. Nelson's regular captain, Miller, remained with Jervis, the *Minerva* being commanded by George Cockburn. The smaller *Blanche* was also put under Nelson's orders, and he was sent to Elba, to be at the service of Sir Gilbert Elliot, who, as Viceroy of Corsica, was in general charge of the area. Elliot was then visiting Italian courts to gather what information he could about their intentions.

Characteristically, his mission led Nelson into a whole series of adventures. On 19 December, while off Cartagena, the *Minerva* and *Blanche* encountered two Spanish frigates, the larger of which, the *Sabina*, was commanded by Don Jacobo Stuart, a descendant of the Duke of Berwick, and thus of James II and Arabella Churchill. Nelson attacked.

I have no idea of a closer or sharper battle [he wrote], the force to a gun the same, and nearly the same number of men, we having two hundred and fifty. I asked him several times to surrender during the action, but

Admiral Sir John Jervis, created Earl of
St Vincent for his victory at Cape St Vincent,
in which Nelson played a vital part.

his answer was, 'No, Sir; not while I have the means of fighting left.' When only he of all the officers was left alive, he hailed, and said he could fight no more, and begged I would stop firing.

Nelson sent a prize crew aboard which included two lieutenants, one of them being Thomas Hardy, but when further Spanish ships arrived on the scene, he was forced to leave his battered conquest. Don Jacobo himself was sent to Spain under a flag of truce, and an exchange of prisoners arranged which would include Hardy. It was conducted in that spirit of courtesy which subsisted between the Navies of Spain and Britain, though not between Britain and France. The *Blanche* also mastered her opponent, but was ordered to rejoin Nelson before she could secure her prize. The *Minerva* had seven men killed and over forty wounded.

On reaching Elba, Nelson found he would have to wait for Elliot, who was at Naples. He sent Fremantle in the *Inconstant* to fetch him, and there Fremantle took the chance to marry Betsey Wynne, a girl of nineteen whose diaries have since delighted many readers. Betsey was under the wing of Sir William and Emma Hamilton ('a beautiful and amiable woman', said the bride of Emma: 'my lady an uncommon treat', Fremantle noted, but on further acquaintance added 'get on tolerably with my lady, whom I dislike'). Fremantle took Betsey on board his frigate, and she was high in favour with Jervis, who once exacted a kiss from her on his own quarter-deck.

The Fremantles rejoined Nelson at Elba, and it was decided to leave a garrison and a frigate at the island, at least for the moment. Other ships in the area, loaded with naval stores, and with Elliot and his Viceroy's suite, sailed for Gibraltar on 29 January 1797, leaving the Fremantles behind. This was the first event of the year in which Nelson achieved public acclaim.

Nelson reconnoitred every important enemy port, including Toulon, on his way to rejoin Jervis. The Viceroy with his despatches and views might be his principal care, but, if he brought news to the Commander-in-Chief of the state and whereabouts of enemy concentrations, it would be of the utmost value. The general belief at the time was that it was the intention of the French, reinforced by a Spanish fleet, to attempt a large-scale invasion. The Brest fleet did in fact make a sortie during the Christmas season, and met with no opposition on its way to Bantry Bay. What defeated French plans, and the hopes of Wolfe Tone, was bad weather. It was that which kept Lord Bridport at anchor at Spithead, a fact which did not increase confidence when news reached the public of what Ireland had escaped.

Near Gibraltar, on his way to Jervis's rendezvous off the Portuguese coast, Nelson was chased by two Spanish ships of the line, one of which sailed faster than the *Minerva*. Hardy was by that time back in the frigate, but at dinner on 11 February there was a cry of 'Man overboard' and he went off instantly in the jolly boat to attempt a rescue. The man was never seen again, but the current in the Straits carried the boat, despite every effort of those at the oars, nearer the enemy, who were almost within gun-shot. At this stage, Nelson exclaimed: 'By God, I'll not lose Hardy! Back the mizen topsail.' The frigate's way was checked, Hardy was picked up, and the Spaniards, suspecting a ruse, shortened sail, allowing the *Minerva* to get away.

Boldness had paid, but it was a narrow shave. A still narrower one occurred after nightfall. Those on deck at one stage discovered the frigate to be in the middle of a fleet which, from the signals observed, was almost certainly Spanish. It was foggy at the time, a circumstance which enabled the *Minerva* to edge away and in due course to head for Jervis with information of the first importance. Without doubt, if Jervis wished, there would be a battle, and everyone knew that his course would be to fight. Collingwood, who was then with him, put the matter well when he wrote home – 'should we not be grateful to him, who had such confidence in his fleet, that he thought no force too great for them?'

The numerical odds against Jervis were indeed heavy. Hardy, from the accident of having visited both Cartagena and Cadiz as a recent prisoner-of-war, was able to confirm and amplify information obtained by Nelson about Spanish strength. Nelson transferred from the *Minerva* back to the *Captain*, now that a general action was imminent. Elliot, together with Colonel Drinkwater of his staff, received permission from Jervis to postpone his urgent passage home until the outcome of the engagement could be known. He and the colonel were entrusted to the care of Lord Garlies, captain of the frigate *Lively*.

It was thus that Drinkwater had the chance of a grandstand view of a naval battle of the first order. It is through him that certain details are known of Nelson's behaviour, and a more experienced eye-witness could scarcely have been found. As a young ensign, Drinkwater had served throughout the memorable siege of Gibraltar, during the War of American Independence, the defence conducted with such distinction by Lord Heathfield. He had

OVERLEAF Commodore Nelson receiving the sword of the defeated and dying Spanish admiral on the quarter deck of the *San Josef*. Nelson boarded the *San Josef* from the *San Nicholas* which he had already taken – 'Nelson's patent bridge for boarding first rates'.

written the classic account of the event. Fifteen years later, he found himself in waters familiar to him, confident that he would witness another triumph of British arms.

Jervis, whose fleet had suffered losses in the Tagus and elsewhere due to stress of weather and other misfortunes, had just been reinforced. He had with him, when the *Minerva* joined, fifteen ships of the line and four frigates. He found himself opposed, when the Spaniards came in sight, by twenty-seven sail of the line, including the largest ship of war in the world, the *Santissima Trinidada*, and ten frigates. His own force was highly trained and disciplined, though many of his ships needed docking. The Spaniards, who were making for Cadiz, but had been driven some way into the Atlantic, were in two loosely organized groups. One of them consisted of fighting ships. The other, to leeward, was a mixed squadron of ships of the line and *urcas*, cargo carriers freighted with quicksilver from the mines near Malaga, a fact of which Jervis was unaware.

Shortly after 11 o'clock on 14 February, Jervis signalled to his fleet, which was by then in line ahead and in close order, that he

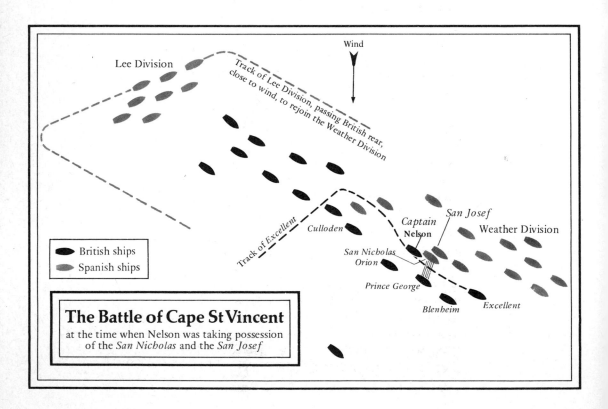

The Battle of Cape St Vincent
at the time when Nelson was taking possession
of the *San Nicholas* and the *San Josef*

intended to sail through the enemy. Soon afterwards, he flew the signal to engage. His flag was in the *Victory*, the line being led by Nelson's old friend and Jervis's favourite captain, Thomas Troubridge, in the *Culloden*. Firing began about 11.30 and Jervis, having effectively divided the Spaniards, ordered his ships to tack in succession, with the idea of concentrating on the body of the enemy, which was to windward. This included the largest ships.

The Spanish admiral, de Cordoba, seeing his danger, tried to counter it by wearing round Jervis's line, in order to join the ships to leeward. He might well have succeeded but for Nelson's initiative. Perceiving Jervis's intention, but seeing also that if he did not act at once, the Spaniards might escape, Nelson ordered his captain, Miller, to wear out of the line and stand on the other tack, heading directly towards the enemy. Jervis once said: 'Hawke, when he ran out of the line ... sickened me of tactics.' He meant that it was just such a manoeuvre as Nelson's, in defiance of strict signals and instructions, that had brought Hawke's first success in battle. It brought Nelson his. The example set by the *Captain* was followed by Collingwood in the *Excellent*, and soon rear-most ships and leading ones were pounding away at the enemy, the others following as best they could. An ordered battle had been turned into a *mêlée*, and this exactly suited the spirit in the British fleet.

Nelson himself wrote a pell-mell account of his share in the day, which he headed, characteristically: '*A few remarks relative to myself in the Captain in which my pendent was flying on the most glorious Valentine's Day 1797*'. The memorandum reads like an old-style adventure story, which is exactly what it was.

... at $\frac{1}{4}$ past one o'clock was engaged with ... the Spanish division, the ships which I know were the *Santissima Trinidada*, 126, *San Nicholas*, 80, another first rate, 112, and 74, names not known. I was immediately joined and most nobly supported by the *Culloden*, Capt. Troubridge. Shortly afterwards the *Salvador del Mundo* and *San Isidro* were fired into in a masterly style by the *Excellent*, Capt. Collingwood, who compelled the *San Isidro* to hoist English colours, and I thought the large ship *Salvador del Mundo* had also struck, but Capt. Collingwood disdaining the parade of taking possession of beaten enemies most gallantly pushed up with every sail set to save his old friend and messmate who to all appearance was in a critical state ... The *Excellent* ranged up within 10 feet of the *San Nicholas* gave a most tremendous fire. The *San Nicholas* luffing up, the *San Josef* fell on board her and the *Excellent* passing on for the *Santissima Trinidada* the *Captain* resumed her situation abreast

The British fleet, with prizes, sails into Lisbon harbour after
the battle of Cape St Vincent. Many ships are jury-rigged
because of battle damage.

74

of them and close alongside. At this time the *Captain* having lost her fore topmast, not a sail, shroud or rope left, her wheel shot away and incapable of further service in the line or in the chase, I directed Capt. Miller to put the helm to starboard and calling for boarders ordered them to board.

The soldiers of the 69th [today the Welsh] Regiment with an alacrity which will ever do them credit and Lieut. Pierson of the same regiment were amongst the foremost on this service. The first man who jumped into the enemy's mizen chains was Capt. Berry late my first lieutenant (Capt. Miller was in the very act of going also but I directed him to remain) he was supported from our sprit sail yard which hooked in the mizen rigging. A soldier of the 69th regiment having broke the upper quarter gallery window jumped in followed by myself and others as fast as possible. I found the cabin doors fastened, and some Spanish officers fired their pistols, but having broke open the doors the soldiers fired and the Spanish brigadier (Commodore with a distinguishing pendant) fell as retreating to the quarter deck on the larboard side near the wheel.

Having pushed on the quarter deck I found Capt. Berry in possession of the poop and the Spanish ensign hauling down. I passed with my people and Lt. Pierson on the larboard gangway to the forecastle where I met two or three Spanish officers, prisoners to my seamen, and they delivered me their swords.

At this moment a fire of pistols or muskets opened from the Admiral's stern gallery of the *San Josef*. I directed the soldiers to fire into her stern and calling to Capt. Miller ordered him to send more men into the *San Nicholas* and directed my people to board the first rate which was done in an instant, Capt. Berry assisting me into the main chains. At this moment a Spanish officer looked over the quarter deck rail and said they surrendered. From this most welcome intelligence it was not long before I was on the quarter deck when the Spanish captain with a bow presented me his sword and said the Admiral was dying of his wounds below. I asked him on his honour if the ship was surrendered. He declared she was, on which I gave him my hand and desired him to call his officers and ship's company and tell them of it which he did, and on the quarter deck of a Spanish first rate, extravagant as the story may seem, did I receive the swords of vanquished Spaniards which as I received I gave to William Fearney one of my barge crew who put them with the greatest sang froid under his arm. I was surrounded by Capt. Berry, Lieut. Pierson, 69th Regiment, John Sykes, John Thompson, Francis Cook, all old Agamemnons and several other brave men, seamen and soldiers. Thus fell these ships.

Jervis, who was created Earl of St Vincent in recognition of his victory, took four prizes all told. At one time the vast *Santissima Trinidada* lowered her flag to Sir James Saumarez, captain of the *Orion*, but was later able to escape. Two prizes had fallen to

Nelson (not by remote control) and he could fairly claim to have had the lion's share on Valentine's Day. He did so claim, and his boasts caused feeling in the Fleet, though not among men such as Collingwood who had not only supported him up to the hilt – Collingwood's gunnery was superlative, as all agreed – but who knew Nelson well enough to understand, and to be sympathetically amused by his self-satisfaction. Such people realized how generous Nelson was to others.

What pleased Nelson as much as anything was to hear that his achievement had been referred to as 'Nelson's Patent Bridge for boarding first-rates'. The feat of capturing a second big ship, from the deck of a first, was unique in a fleet action. As for his enlightened 'disobedience', Jervis received him with open arms after the battle, when he appeared, still grimy, with a nasty bruise in his groin, and with part of his hat missing, on the quarter-deck of the flag-ship. He had previously confided to Drinkwater, who had said they would probably make him a baronet, that this would not suit him at all. He had not the means to maintain an hereditary title.

Placing his hand on my arm [wrote the colonel], and looking me most expressively in the face, he said, 'No, no: if they want to mark my services, it must not be in that manner.' 'Oh!' said I, interrupting him, 'you wish to be made a Knight of the Bath . . .' My supposition proved correct, for he instantly answered me, 'Yes: if my services have been of any value, let them be noticed in a way that the public may know me – or them' . . . He wished to bear about his person some honorary distinction, to attract the public eye, and mark his professional services.

Thanks to Sir Gilbert Elliot saying a word or two in the right quarter, it was arranged as Nelson wished, and every flag officer and captain also received a gold medal from the King. By that time, Nelson had become a Rear Admiral by seniority, happy timing in view of his services at sea.

There were periods in Nelson's life about which it is almost irresistible to comment: 'If only he had gone home at this stage, what a lot he would have been spared.' The spring of 1797 was one of them, for the summer brought many trials. At home, Lord Bridport's fleet mutinied at Spithead, refusing to put to sea until grievances were remedied. These included pay, which was derisory even by the standards of the age; victualling; care of the sick. There were scores of others, though the ringleaders did not lay stress on the shattering punishments inflicted at the will or

Jolly Jack Tar – Romance and Reality

The romantic view of a sailor's life as exemplified in song and verse (*overleaf*) was far from the reality. More often than not, men were forced into naval service by brutal press gangs (*below*); conditions on board were poor; diet restricted; shore leave curtailed; the lash always threatening. The rewards of this harsh existence were scant. Pay was poor and the amount of prize money paid for action at sea was derisory for the men considering the dangers involved and the injuries sustained. There was often difficulty in collecting prize money from the agents, as this contemporary caricature (*right*) by Rowlandson illustrates.

I. Hearty from Leverpool.

C Moſley Sculp.

The Sailor's Return.

Juſt on the Beach arriv'd, with great Surprize,
Jack ſees his Molly; Him too **Molly** ſpies;
What! is it Thou? with open Arms ſhe cries,
Then drops the brittle Goods ſhe ſells for Bread,
While all aghaſt beſide ſtands Meſsmate **Ned**,
And points where flows the Bowl, & Gen'rous Red.

But **Molly's** Mother, more ſagacious, opes
The wealthy Cheſt, on which ſhe plac'd her hopes,
And for the richeſt Prizes careful gropes.
The ſettled Crew gay Mirth and Love proclaim;
One leads aloft the mercenary Dame,
Who drunk, returns her Load from whence it came.

Contemning Wealth, which they with Riſk obtain,
Thus Sailors love, and then to Sea again.

Printed for Carington Bowles   in St. Pauls Church Yard, London.

whim of captains. It was common ground how much they contributed to the misery, fear and hazard of life in the Navy. 'Our Fleets,' wrote Admiral Vernon earlier in the century, 'are defrauded by injustice, manned by violence, and maintained by cruelty.' Every syllable was true. The country depended on the Fleet as never before, and if the men were ever to be better treated, then was the time to press their case. Unfortunately, a more serious outbreak at the Nore, after grievances had already in some measure at least been attended to, robbed the men of sympathy, and St Vincent had a short way with troublemakers whenever they appeared in his command. He once hanged four of them – and on a Sunday.

Jervis soon had another Mediterranean mission for Nelson, which might have seemed at the time a final measure. Early in April he sent him to Elba to superintend withdrawal. The Government saw no point in keeping troops on the island. When Nelson returned to the Fleet, he hoisted his flag in the *Theseus*, taking Miller with him from the *Captain*. The *Theseus* was not long out from England, and her men were unruly. Betsey Fremantle, whose husband was then in the *Seahorse*, a successor to the ship which years earlier had taken Nelson to India, remarked 'the *Theseus* men the most tiresome noisy mutinous people in the world, they annoyed me amazingly, and Fremantle still more'. Nelson, however, rarely had trouble with his crews, and before long a paper was found on the quarter-deck which read:

Success attend Admiral Nelson God bless Captain Miller we thank them for the officers they have placed over us. We are happy and comfortable and will shed every drop of blood in our veins to support them, and the name of the *Theseus* shall be immortalised as high as the *Captain*'s ship's company.

This was one of the many tributes Nelson received during his life from the lower deck. The men were as good as their word during the heavy inshore fighting which now took place close to Cadiz, where Nelson was in charge, Fremantle being with him. Nevertheless, the mutinies at home encouraged a stiffening in Nelson's attitude towards indiscipline, and there were occasions in the future when he would punish mercilessly.

Meanwhile, he and Fremantle continued to share adventures, one of them being related by Nelson in the summary of his life with which he supplied the editors of the *Naval Chronicle*. On

3 July there occurred an episode during which, in the admiral's own words:

... perhaps my personal courage was more conspicuous than at any other period of my life. In an attack of the Spanish gun-boats, I was boarded in my barge with its common crew of ten men, Cockswain, Captain Fremantle and myself, by the Commander of the gun-boats. The Spanish barge rowed twenty-six oars, besides officers, thirty in the whole; this was a service hand-to-hand with swords, in which my Cockswain, John Sykes (now no more) twice saved my life. Eighteen of the Spaniards being killed and several wounded, we succeeded in taking their Commander.

Fremantle got cut around the face, but made light of it when he returned to Betsey in the *Seahorse*. What she noted in her diary was: 'I was anxious for Fremantle and did not go to bed till he returned. Spanish gun boats and a barge were taken, many people killed and wounded. Fremantle received a blow.' Little more than a week later, Nelson sailed for Santa Cruz, Teneriffe, in the hope of capturing a treasure ship from Spanish America which was believed to have put in to the Canaries on her way home. The *Seahorse* formed part of his force, and Betsey accompanied her husband. The gallant and efficient Troubridge was second in command.

Nelson's force consisted of three ships of the line, three frigates and a cutter. He sailed on 15 July, with everyone in high hopes of prize money. Nelson, who read history, knew all about Blake's brilliantly successful raid on Santa Cruz in 1657, and hoped to emulate his feat, though he told St Vincent he did not reckon himself Blake's equal.

Islands had never been propitious for him. His attack on Turks Island as a young captain had been a fiasco. The campaign in Corsica had cost him the sight of an eye. Teneriffe was the most disastrous venture of all, and from the outset nothing went right.

Troubridge landed on 22 July, but his men had to be withdrawn, dead with fatigue, with nothing done. Shoal water prevented the ships getting in close enough to the shore to silence the batteries, and the only chance of success now seemed to be a night attack. This was made at 2 a.m. on 25 July, and was led by Nelson in person. The surf was high: the Spaniards were prepared, and the boats lost their way. Heavy fire cost many casualties, some 250 officers and men being killed and the cutter sunk. Only the resource of Troubridge saved him from having to capitulate. He threatened to burn down the town, and made his own terms with

82

Nelson's confidence in the worth of his 'brave fellows' was amply returned by their idolization of him.

His Honor Lord Nelson to be sure -- so here is his good health and the Wooden Walls of Old England

What do you think of that there Master Solomons our Chaplain palavers so much about

King Solomon you mean -- why bless your simple head if King Solomon was alive now -- the times are so strangely alter'd -- I dont think he could tell a Gib boom. from a poop Lanthern.

AILORS in ARGUMENT..

Etch'd by Robert

Pub'd by R. Roberts No. 28 Middle Row Holborn

Islands were never lucky for Nelson –
it was while taking part in
an abortive attack on Santa Cruz,
Teneriffe that his arm was so badly
wounded it had to be amputated.

84

a chivalrous opponent. The British were allowed to embark in good order; compliments were exchanged; and Nelson returned to St Vincent a chastened man. He was also badly wounded, and so was Fremantle.

Nelson was shot in the right arm as he stepped ashore. Josiah, who had been made a lieutenant three months before, saved his step-father's life by his resource, and it was perhaps the finest hour he was to know. Fanny later wrote down what she remembered of his account. It was composed in a breathless style suited to the event.

Lieut. N. took off his hat in order to catch the blood and feeling where the bones were broken he grasped the arm with one hand which stopped the bleeding, the revolting of the blood was so great that Sir H. said he would never forget it and he tied up his arm and placed him as comfortably as he could with his two silk neckerchiefs from his throat, and then found one Lovel a seaman and 5 other sailors to assist in rowing him off.

When the boat reached the side of the ship Nisbet called out 'Tell the surgeon the Admiral is wounded and he must prepare for amputation,' upon which they offered to let down the chair, Sir H. Nelson said 'No I have yet my legs and one arm,' and he walked up the side of the ship, Lieut. N. keeping so close that in case he slipped he could have caught him.

On getting on the quarter deck the officers as usual saluted him by taking off their hats, which compliment Nelson returned with his left hand as if nothing had happened. Lovel took off his shirt and gave him slips to tie the poor arm round his neck.

Nelson said in ten minutes more he was no more.

Fremantle's wound, also in the arm, did not lead to amputation, but it pained and troubled him longer than Nelson's more serious damage. It happened that the surgeon on board the *Theseus*, Thomas Eshelby, who had the help of Louis Remonier, a royalist refugee from Toulon, had more skill than most such men who served in the Navy, so that Nelson could be accounted lucky. As early as 29 July, Eshelby was able to report '... stump looked well. No bad symptom whatever occurred. The sore reduced to the size of a shilling. In perfect health. One of the ligatures not come away.'

The ligature troubled Nelson for months, but otherwise he made an astonishing recovery. He had much to occupy him, despatches to dictate, fellow casualties to cheer up: and a mere two days after his amputation, he sent a line to Betsey, shakily but legibly left-handed – 'God Bless you and Fremantle.'

The saw with which
Nelson's arm was amputated.

On 16 August, still on board the *Theseus*, Nelson wrote to
St Vincent:

I rejoice at being once more in sight of your flag and with your permission will come on board the *Ville de Paris* and pay you my respects . . .
A left handed Admiral will never again be considered as useful therefore
the sooner I get to a very humble cottage the better, and make room for
a better man to serve the State. . . .

St Vincent could be at his best in such disappointing circumstances. Far from blaming Nelson, he was all sympathy. He
listened to Nelson's explanation of the defeat, commented that
'mortals cannot command success, but you and your companions
have certainly deserved it', pooh-poohed any idea that his subordinate's usefulness had ended because he had lost a limb; gave
Josiah charge of a ship with the rank of commander, and sent
Nelson home in the *Seahorse*, with the Fremantles, to convalesce.
Dr Eshelby transferred to the frigate, which was helpful to both
the wounded captains.

Betsey reported Nelson to be in great spirits on the way up
Channel, but remarked that it 'looks shocking to be without one
arm'. She was carrying her first child, and feeling its effects, but
she was a happy woman, and she remained so.

By Friday 1 September, the *Seahorse* had anchored at Spithead.
Nelson was rowed ashore, setting foot in England for the first time
in more than four years. He went straight to Bath, where he felt
sure of finding Fanny, and, perhaps, his father. He had said he
would one day 'come laughing home' and he was as good as his
word.

In spite of the pain his arm continued to give him until the
beginning of December, when he 'returned thanks to Almighty

OPPOSITE One of the first
written with his left hand,
this letter to St Vincent
expresses his fears that
his naval career is at an end.

86

Theseus, Aug.t 16.th 1797,

My Dear Sir,

Rejoice at being once more
in sight of your flag, and with your per=
=mission will come on board the Ville de Paris & pay
you my respects. If the Emerald has joined, you
know my wishes, a left handed Admiral will
never again be considered as useful therefore
the sooner I get to a very humble cottage the better
and make room for a better man to serve the State
but whatever be my lot Believe me with the most
sincere affection Your most faithful
                                    Horatio Nelson
    Turn over

God for his perfect recovery from a severe wound', the months which Nelson spent in England at this time were among the most refreshing he ever enjoyed. Certainly for Fanny they represented fulfilment such as she had not yet known during her second marriage. In the years when Nelson had been ashore on half pay, he had been restless, eager to resume his professional career. But his absence had so fretted her that, when she heard of his exploits off Cape St Vincent, she had begged him, with a certain ironic humour, to 'leave boarding to *Captains*'. Now he had become a national hero, with a star on his coat which gave him immense pleasure. It was to become a feature of the portrait commissioned from Lemuel Francis Abbott.

Even more encouraging, he was well treated by the authorities, who granted him a wound pension of £800 a year, and he had firm assurances from both Lord St Vincent and the Admiralty, where Lord Spencer presided, that an active command would be given him when the doctors pronounced him fit. When the Nelsons dined at the Admiralty, placed next to one another so that Fanny could cut up her husband's meat, Lady Spencer noted that Nelson treated his wife like a lover.

It was true that the war itself was still going badly. For instance, the Bank of England had suspended cash payments, and when Sir Gilbert Elliot and Colonel Drinkwater had returned with first news of the sea victory in February, they could hardly scrape enough cash in the West Country to provide for their journey to London. But in October, Adam Duncan, with a scratch force, including ships which had recently mutinied, won a splendid victory over the Dutch at Camperdown. Nelson was so delighted on hearing the news that he declared he would have given his other arm to be there.

One final discomfiture in the European scene was that, although the victories of St Vincent and Camperdown had settled any immediate threat of invasion, Portugal had made peace with France. It was therefore doubtful how much longer the British fleet could make use of the Tagus anchorages. A Mediterranean sortie seemed more necessary than ever, this time with objects which included the capture of Minorca, with its fine harbour at Port Mahon, and the discovery of the purpose behind the huge efforts being made by France in all her own southern ports, and those she controlled, to arm and equip a sea-borne expedition.

Lord St Vincent wished for Nelson's return as being the most active flag officer he knew. It would, so he told Lord Spencer, give

him new heart. He had not long to wait. The *Vanguard*, a 74-gun ship, was commissioned for Nelson's flag as a Rear Admiral of the Blue. The flag was hoisted at Spithead on 29 March 1798.

It was then usual for junior post captains to be appointed to flag-ships, where they could be under the experienced eye of a superior. Edward Berry, who had had a Norfolk education, had been Nelson's first lieutenant in the *Agamemnon* and served as a volunteer on board the *Captain* while holding the rank of commander, had recently been promoted for his services in boarding the Spanish ships on Valentine's Day. Like Nelson, he was one of a large family; he was liked by Fanny; and he knew Nelson's ways. Although never a prudent officer, he was full of dash, and was proverbial for his luck in being on the spot whenever a fight was on. It was not an ideal appointment, since a man of less volatile

Nelson's ingenious combined knife and fork.

OVERLEAF Much of the practical burden of Nelson's disability must have fallen upon the shoulders of his personal servant at sea, Tom Allen, a Burnham Thorpe man.

temperament might have served Nelson even better. Certainly Nelson had some difficulty in settling into his new ship. His luggage was badly packed; he lived at first in great discomfort, and he soon realized the handicap which wounds brought with them. He left England in less high spirits than when he arrived, and it was clear that his Burnham Thorpe servant, Tom Allen, had much to learn if he wished to make his master comfortable.

5 The Nile

Pub. Oct. 6th 1798. by H. Humphrey 27 St. Jamess Street

Extirpation of the Plagues of Egypt;—Destruction of Revolu

Crocodiles;—or—The British Hero cleansing ye Mouth of ye Nile.

THE *Vanguard*, with a convoy to protect, arrived at Lisbon on 23 April, where Nelson found Josiah, who had command of the hospital ship, *Dolphin*. He was not pleased with his stepson or his ship, and he hoped the young man would soon be given a frigate. A week later, Nelson was off Cadiz, where he joined Lord St Vincent. The Commander-in-Chief wrote to Lord Spencer next day:

... the arrival of Admiral Nelson has given me new life: you could not have gratified me more than in sending him; his presence in the Mediterranean is so very essential that I mean to put the *Orion* and *Alexander* under his command, with the addition of three or four Frigates and to send him away ... to endeavour to ascertain the real object of the preparations making by the French.

St Vincent, who habitually used a tone of the sharpest realism in speaking of those under his command, had his officers in strict control, but there were restless spirits among them, and one flag officer, Sir John Orde, became so jealous on learning that Nelson was chosen for the Mediterranean foray that he actually challenged his superior to a duel, which was forbidden by the King.

As for the *Orion* and the *Alexander*, 'the Earl', as Nelson sometimes called him, could not have picked on finer ships and captains. The *Orion* was in charge of the very senior Sir James Saumarez, who had had an even more remarkable career than Nelson. He had been one of Rodney's captains at his victory of 1782, and had been knighted for a brilliant frigate action eleven years later. He and Nelson were not close, as were their wives, but, after seeing Nelson in action at Cape St Vincent, Saumarez had written home: 'Be not surprised if, with our desperate Commodore, you hear of our taking the whole Spanish fleet, should we fall in with them.' Captain Ball of the *Alexander* was to become one of Nelson's dearest friends. They had met once, years before, at St Omer, when Nelson thought Ball a bit of a coxcomb. That view soon changed.

The opening moves of the re-entry into the Mediterranean were not propitious. The weather was bad, and by the end of May, Nelson's command could scarcely be termed even a Squadron of Observation, for the flag-ship had been dismasted and the frigates were dispersed, never to regain touch, for they returned to Gibraltar. On 24 May, from Sardinia, Nelson sent his wife a letter which so struck those who read it that Fanny was asked for copies by friends, including Sir Gilbert Elliot, now Lord Minto, and Lord Spencer:

PREVIOUS PAGES *The British hero cleanses the mouth of the Nile* – a Gillray cartoon.

My Dearest Fanny,

I ought not to call what has happened to the *Vanguard* by the cold name of accident, I believe firmly that it was the Almighty's goodness to check my consummate vanity. I hope it has made me a better officer, as I feel confident it has made me a better man. I kiss with all humility the rod.

Figure to yourself a vain man on Sunday evening at sunset walking in his cabin with a squadron about him who looked up to their chief to lead them to glory and in whom this chief placed the firmest reliance that the proudest ships in equal numbers belonging to France would have bowed their flags, and with a very rich prize lying by him.

Figure to yourself this proud conceited man, when the sun rose on Monday morning, his ship dismasted, his fleet dispersed and himself in such distress that the meanest frigate out of France would have been a very unwelcome guest.

But it has pleased Almighty God to bring us into a safe port, where altho' we are refused the rights of humanity, yet the *Vanguard* will in two days get to sea again as an Englishman of war. The exertions of Sir James Saumarez and Captain Ball have been wonderful, and if the ship had been in England, months would have been taken to send her to sea. Here my operations will not be delayed four days, and I shall join the rest of my fleet on the rendezvous ... We are all health and good humour. Tell Lady Saumarez Sir James never was in better health. . . .

There followed a list of damage to masts, yards, bowsprit and other equipment. Nelson had one young man killed in the storm and several seamen hurt: but the resource of Saumarez and Ball was applied to repair with such skill that by the time the 'rest of the fleet' had joined, all the more serious damage had been made good. It was a striking instance of how, in the days of sail, given the necessary activity a squadron could keep operational without any of the usual dockyard facilities.

It had always been St Vincent's intention to send some of his best 74-gun ships to join Nelson, the moment reinforcements arrived from home. He even spared Troubridge, and would have preferred him to have been Nelson's second in command rather than Saumarez. When the force joined Nelson, which it did on 7 June, he had possibly the finest fleet ever assembled under sail – fourteen ships of the line, the *Vanguard, Orion, Culloden, Bellerophon, Minotaur, Defence, Alexander, Zealous, Audacious, Goliath, Theseus, Majestic, Swiftsure* and *Leander*. The *Leander*, however, mounted 50 guns only, and the *Mutine*, brig, with Hardy in command, was the sole ship capable of scouting, since St Vincent had been unable to spare any more frigates. This was Nelson's greatest handicap in the anxious weeks ahead.

Anxious they were, because although Nelson knew that the French armada was ready, he had no information about its destination. But as Bonaparte was with it, it was obviously of the first importance. Naples – Malta – Sicily – Egypt – an invasion of Britain: all were possibilities. Then news came, that the enemy had been seen off Sicily. Troubridge went in Hardy's brig to Naples, to gather what news he could from Sir William Hamilton. It was not much: but on 22 June Nelson learnt that Malta had been surrendered by the Knights of St John, who were largely pro-French, after only a token show of resistance.

Nelson thought nothing of Councils of War, but as a responsible flag officer, concerned with what next to do, accompanied by captains of long experience, he sent them a questionnaire asking their views about where the enemy were likely to be heading. Ball said Alexandria; so did Berry (which suggested that Nelson's

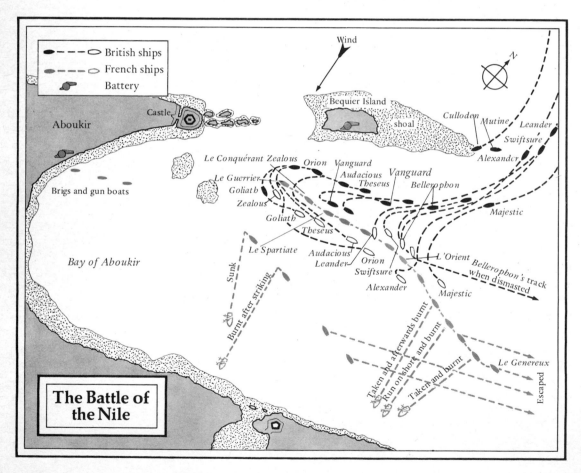

The Battle of the Nile

own inclination was that way); Darby of the *Bellerophon*, Saumarez and Troubridge all agreed. Nelson set sail for the Egyptian port, but wrote a series of agonized letters to St Vincent. In forwarding copies to Spencer, the Commander-in-Chief remarked that they were 'not fit for the eye of a gossiping Board', adding that 'it is proper your Lordship should see the inmost recesses of such a soul as Nelson's'.

The captains were right. Bonaparte was indeed making for Alexandria and it is an indication of how well Nelson's ships kept together, but how badly they needed look-out frigates, that the British and French fleets missed each other completely, though the French thought they heard British signal guns one night. Nelson reached Alexandria on 28 June, found the port empty, and returned to Sicily, baffled. His top-sails had scarcely disappeared over the horizon when the first French ships arrived, and Bonaparte was able to land his army unopposed.

At Syracuse, where his fleet watered and provisioned, Nelson had the happy intuition, since no reports had come in of the French having reversed course, which might have suggested invasion or an attack on Naples, to lead his force back to Egypt. His dilemma had one good result. During much of June and the whole of July he had been given the chance to take his captains fully into his confidence, to make them aware of his tactical ideas under any given circumstances, to make them feel that they were free to use their initiative.

On first returning to Egypt, it seemed that disappointment again awaited Nelson. Saumarez wrote:

When on the morning of the 1st of August the reconnoitring ship made the signal that the enemy was not there, despondency nearly took possession of my mind, and I do not recollect ever to have felt so utterly hopeless, or out of spirits, as when we sat down to dinner; judge then what a change took place when, as the cloth was being removed, the officer of the watch hastily came in, saying: 'Sir, a signal is just now made that the enemy *is* in Aboukir Bay, and moored in a line of battle.' All sprang from their seats, and only staying to drink a bumper to our success, we were in a moment on deck. On our appearance there, the men, animated by one spirit, gave three hearty cheers, in token of their joy at having at length found their looked-for enemy, without the possibility of his again eluding their pursuit.

The French position, in fact, looked strong enough. Brueys, the fleet commander, had mounted a battery on Aboukir Island; there were shoals and sandbanks which made navigation hazardous, and the very idea that the British, who, when first sighted, were in loose formation, would at once form line of battle and sail in to the attack, would have seemed to most admirals the height of rashness and improbability. Brueys had parties watering ashore, and at first had some hesitation in recalling them. There was no hesitation of any sort on Nelson's part. His early mentor, Hawke, had taken 'Strike' for his motto. That was what Nelson did, and upon the instant. He directed his 'band of brothers' to bear down upon the French.

The leading captain, Foley, sailing the *Goliath* into the bay, decided that where there was room for a Frenchman to anchor, there might also be room for an opponent to work inshore of him, and to expose him to fire on the side for which he would not have been prepared. He was right, and his action, as brilliant in initiative and as justified by results as anything even in Nelson's own career, was followed by four other captains, including Saumarez. This made sure that part of the French line was doubled — two ships opposing one. Nelson himself, with his remaining force — all but the *Culloden*, which stuck on a sandbank and nearly drove Troubridge crazy — went in from the seaward side. From a little after six o'clock, throughout the rest of that soft summer night, the slowly advancing British ships battered and blasted the French one by one until the gunners lay down beside their smoking pieces, overcome with exhaustion.

The most awe-inspiring moment in the battle came long after nightfall, when the French flag-ship, *L'Orient*, her holds crammed with spoils from Malta, suddenly caught fire. After blazing fiercely for about an hour, she blew up, and with so deafening an explosion that it startled troops in Alexandria, fifteen miles away. The shock was such that, in the words of Captain Berry 'there was an awful pause and death-like silence for about three minutes'. Brueys himself died in the flames after sustaining many wounds, and the greater number of his officers and men also perished, including the Chief of Staff, Commodore Bianca, and his young son, who became the subject of romantic song:

> The boy stood on the burning deck
> When all but he had fled . . .

This lends itself too easily to parody, but there was indeed more than one incident of herosim in the last moments of the flag-ship.

The sight next morning defied description. 'Victory,' wrote Nelson to Fanny, 'is certainly not a name strong enough for such

Captain Foley of the Goliath, whose brilliant opening manoeuvre set the stage for the victory of the Nile.

a scene as I have passed.' His effective ships had reduced eleven of the line and two frigates to smoking hulks, every one of them flying the British flag above the Tricolour. Only two ships of the line and two frigates escaped, and in one of them was Villeneuve, who was to cross swords with Nelson again in his last battle. Not even Villeneuve would have got away had any British ship been in a position to chase. Nearly all were seriously damaged. One, the *Bellerophon*, had been completely dismasted by *L'Orient*, and

An awesome moment in the
battle – the night sky is
illuminated as *L'Orient*
explodes after burning for
an hour. It was the death
of a young boy in this
inferno which inspired the
lines 'the boy stood on
the burning deck . . .'

Nelson's head injury is dressed in the cockpit of the *Vanguard* during the battle of the Nile.

all her officers were killed or wounded. The ship was saved by the courage of her gunner, Richard Hindmarsh, who lost the sight of an eye but survived to attain knighthood and flag rank.

Nelson himself had not escaped. During the height of the battle, he had been hit in the forehead with a fragment of iron shot. The wound temporarily blinded him altogether, and seemed at first so grave that he thought he was dying. Even so, he refused to be attended to before what he called his 'brave fellows' – men who had been wounded earlier – had had their turn. The surgeon soon convinced him that, although painful and messy, his was no mortal injury, and he was led on deck to see the last of the blazing *L'Orient*. Even before firing had ceased he began dictating a despatch which was to ring through Europe: 'Almighty God has blessed His Majesty's arms in the late Battle by a great Victory over the Fleet of the Enemy, who I attacked at sunset on 1st August at the mouth of the Nile.'

When the news of Nelson's exploit at length reached London,

102

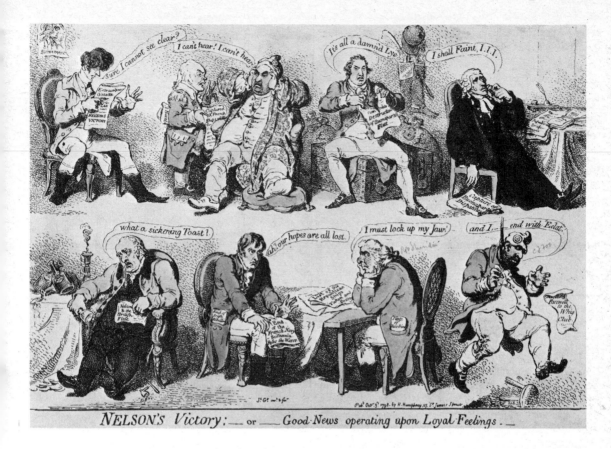

NELSON'S *Victory:* — or — *Good News operating upon Loyal Feelings.* —

the excitement was such that the First Lord of the Admiralty fell flat on the floor outside his room in Whitehall. Lady Spencer wrote to Nelson saying that she was 'half mad' with joy at hearing of such a staggering blow to the enemy. She was not alone. There had been nothing more remarkable at sea within memory: and Nelson later wrote to Lord Howe, *doyen* of British admirals, to say that he thought that, but for his own wound, it would have been total – not a French ship would have escaped. He believed he could have animated his battle-weary officers and men somehow or other to complete the business.

At last the French, including Bonaparte, had met with a reverse which no amount of propaganda, however skilful, and no official silence on their part, could hope to disguise. England rang with praise, and even *The Times* referred to the victor as 'Lord' Nelson before the King had bestowed a peerage upon him.

Few incidents in Nelson's life illustrate better how fitted he was for high command than an action he took almost as soon as the

Published as the news reached London of Nelson's victory, this cartoon depicts the consternation with which Pitt's political opponents greeted the inevitable strengthening of his government.

103

battle was over, and when he was still suffering from the concussion caused by his head wound. He chose an officer to go at once to India, through a Turkish port and an overland route, to inform the East India Company that the immediate threat to their territory had been removed. It would, he knew, save the officials both anxiety and expense. The Company showed appropriate gratitude by voting Nelson a gift of £10,000. It was not for nothing that he had served an early commission in Far Eastern waters. As a result, he had a world-picture always in his mind, an essential ingredient in a strategist, though one not possessed by every admiral of his time.

The large and advancing French army in Egypt was now cut off, isolated from the Mother Country and indeed from the Continent in general. Great Britain had not merely re-entered the Mediterranean — henceforth, and for the remainder of the war, she dominated it. A blockade of Malta and Alexandria was at once established and although, a year later, Napoleon himself evaded the seaward watch and got away from Egypt with a few picked officers in a Venetian-built frigate, the ultimate failure of his expedition had been assured by a few hours fighting at sea.

Besides giving immense help to Pitt in organizing a new coalition against France, the main supports of which were to be Austria and Russia, Nelson hoped to be able to act further against the enemy at once, through the Neapolitans. As soon as his ships were in a reasonable state of repair, he took a squadron to Naples where, after an unparalleled personal reception, he inspired the lazy and sport-mad King Ferdinand to attempt a move upon Rome, which had been occupied by a French force. Ferdinand would be supported from seaward by Nelson.

Much which was unfortunate happened to Nelson during the two years within which he was drawn into the orbit of the Sicilian court. The weeks immediately after the battle of the Nile are foremost among those when admirers of his finer qualities wish he had gone home, as at one stage seems to have been his intention. Yet, there were sound considerations which led him to Naples, and equally good reasons why he should have sent Saumarez with the prizes to Gibraltar.

Victory in itself was all very fine, but Nelson knew, better than most commanders, that the highest test of success was the way it was followed up. In this respect, some of the greater admirals, including Rodney and Howe, had on occasion been lacking. In their case, the reason had been age and weariness. Nelson was

OPPOSITE Nelson successfully attacks a much larger Spanish launch during the bombardment of Cadiz in which he served in July 1797.

104

John Bull taking a Luncheon: or British Cooks cramming Old Grumble-Gizzard with Bonne-Chère. The growing power of the Royal Navy admirably caricatured by Gillray in October 1798.

weary, and suffering much from his head wound, but he was young – under forty at the time of the battle – exceptionally resilient, and with a strategical sense which, though less evident than his qualities as a tactician, showed him in plain terms where his immediate duty lay.

Naples was indeed the likeliest immediate ally. The Queen's mother was Empress of Austria, and the Queen herself, Maria Carolina, detested the French, who had guillotined her sister, Marie Antoinette. Sir William Hamilton, the British Minister, though no longer young, had served as a Guards officer in a brilliant period for the army, and had already written off to St Vincent, full of ideas. The Prime Minister, Sir John Acton, was an expatriate English Catholic.

Sir William's wife, Emma, who was then in ripe maturity, proved to be a tireless feeder of Nelson's vanity, and she might well have turned the head of a man less dependent than he was on comforts which she delighted to supply. Not the least of her virtues, in Nelson's eyes, was that she was tolerant of the uncouth Josiah. The young man had indeed been given a frigate by St Vincent, but was proving a bad captain.

But from the start, no military scheme went right. Nelson, who could well have recalled the limitations of Neapolitan soldiers from his experience at Toulon five years earlier, found that, although spirited when advancing against no opposition, they had only to come up against French garrisons to show their worth. Ferdinand's stay at Rome was brief. He, his army, and his Austrian general, Mack, were soon in full retreat to Naples. The King was popular with the bulk of his subjects, and a citizen army might have defended the capital against a French invasion – but he gave it no chance to do so. Ferdinand, his Queen, his family and Court, decided that Sicily was the place to winter. They fled there in Nelson's ships, the holds stuffed with treasure, only to meet with a December storm in which one of the royal children died in Emma Hamilton's arms, and Sir William was found in a cabin holding a pistol, declaring he preferred to shoot himself, if it came to a choice, rather than to drown. Nelson anchored at Palermo at Christmas 1798, and the most glorious year of his life ended in fiasco.

The following year, 1799, was sombre. To employ a word used by Addison, a writer Nelson favoured, the course of Nelson's life became 'implex' – changing from good to bad and sometimes the other way about. Much of his time was spent in Sicily, with

OPPOSITE Two aspects of the battle of the Nile. ABOVE The preternatural calm of fleet ranged ready for battle in Aboukir Bay. BELOW The fury of action at 6.30 pm.

RIGHT King Ferdinand IV and Queen
Maria Carolina of Naples – a miniature
from a snuffbox. They were very fond of
Emma Hamilton (*left*, in an Italianite
attitude) and she of them. In 1798, the
royal family and the Hamiltons fled from
Naples in Nelson's ships, and, during
a storm at sea, the infant Prince Albert
died in Emma's arms. This mourning
locket (*below*) containing a lock of his
hair belonged to her.

excursions elsewhere. The general news from Europe continued unfavourable to the Allied cause, and Nelson deemed it his duty to protect Ferdinand from the worst consequences of the campaign on the mainland. Concurrently, he had the administration of his force to attend to, and this without a staff.

Immediately after the battle of the Nile, he had sent Captain Berry home with his despatches in the *Leander*, promoting Hardy out of the *Mutine* into the *Vanguard* in Berry's place. Unfortunately, the *Leander* had been intercepted by the *Généreux*, one of the two French ships of the line which had escaped from Aboukir Bay. Thompson, the *Leander*'s captain, ably backed by Berry, put up a stiff fight, but a 50-gun ship was no match for a 74, and the *Leander* was forced to surrender. The French pillaged her, and the two captains were lucky to be exchanged shortly afterwards. Both were knighted for their gallantry. Duplicate despatches reached Europe safely in the *Mutine*, which was put in charge of Nelson's best lieutenant, William Hoste.

Hardy's promotion, which had been as quick as Berry's, meant that Nelson had no officer about him of seniority and experience constantly at his side, for Troubridge was on detached service. Hardy was a fine seaman, and a ruthless disciplinarian, a 'taut

OPPOSITE Nelson, sketched at Naples after the battle of the Nile.
BELOW Captain Hardy's snuffbox, engraved with his name, the *Vanguard*'s, and the year he took command of her.

The bay of Naples with
Vesuvius erupting.

114

A BORDO IL FULMINANTE
29. Giugno 1799.

ONorato Lord Nelſon Ammiraglio della Flotta Brittanica nella rada di Napoli da notizia a tutti quelli che hanno ſervito da Officiali nel Militare, e nelle cariche civili l'infame ſedicente Repubblica Napoletana, che ſe ſi ritrovano nel circuito della Città di Napoli debbano in termine di 24. ore preſentarſi ai Comandanti del Caſtellonuovo, o del Caſtello dell'Ovo, fidandoſi alla clemenza di S. M. Siciliana, e ſe ſi ritrovano nelle vicinanze di detta Città fino alla diſtanza di cinque miglia debbano egualmente preſentarſi ai detti Comandanti, ma in termine di 48. ore ; altrimenti ſaranno conſiderati dal ſudetto Ammiraglio Lord Nelſon come ribelli, ed inimici della preſata M. S. Siciliana.

Nelson's proclamation to the citizens of Naples,
giving the Republicans twenty-four hours to surrender.

OPPOSITE Lady Hamilton as Ariadne, by Romney.

hand' if ever there was one. But he had no control over Nelson, and he was not the sort of man to carry weight with the Hamiltons. His business was with the *Vanguard*. Nelson, living ashore, became immersed in Neapolitan affairs, and was soon the slave of Emma, a bondage which endured for the rest of his days.

During the course of the summer, there was a threat to the British position in the Mediterranean owing to the sortie of a French fleet from Brest, commanded by Bruix. Bridport's system of watch once more let him down, and Collingwood, who was then a Rear Admiral and with the Channel Fleet, described Bruix's escape as 'horrible bungling work'. Nelson was ordered to cruise with the idea of intercepting the French, and he was at sea until it seemed that Bruix presented no immediate threat to Naples, Sicily, Malta, which the British were blockading, or Egypt. He then returned to Palermo, where on 21 June he embarked both the Hamiltons. With them, he proceeded to Naples, with authority from King Ferdinand to act as his plenipotentiary.

Six months of French occupation had been disastrous. The French had made themselves detested, and Cardinal Ruffo, a local warrior-cleric of great ability, had organized an army in Ferdinand's southerly mainland provinces. He had advanced with such success that French garrisons, surrounded in the Castles of Uovo and Nuovo and elsewhere, capitulated. When he arrived in the bay of Naples on 25 June, Nelson annulled a truce agreed to by Ruffo and intimated to all Neapolitan collaborators that they must submit to the mercy of their Sovereign, Ferdinand, who was careful enough of his own skin not to embark for his principal capital until he was sure he was in no danger. Even then, he did not trust himself ashore.

Before the King's arrival, Nelson, who was flying his flag in the *Foudroyant*, a brand new ship just out from home, had acted with extreme severity towards Admiral Caraccioli, a collaborator who had been seized and brought on board. Nelson ordered his immediate trial by a court of Neapolitan officers. The result was a foregone conclusion, and the wretched man was executed on board a Sicilian frigate. This was indeed summary justice, and Nelson could hardly have been surprised, though he continued to be indignant, when his actions were criticized after reports reached England.

The attitude Nelson adopted at Naples, and the odium he brought upon himself, was made worse by his refusal to obey orders sent by Lord Keith, who had now replaced St Vincent as Commander-

116

in-Chief, to detach ships to Minorca, which Keith believed to be threatened. Nelson's forces were dispersed aiding the Neapolitans and blockading the French, and he did not believe Minorca to be in danger. Although he was right in his judgement, the reprimand he received was in every way justified.

After a visit lasting until 5 August, Nelson left Naples with Ferdinand aboard the flag-ship. He arrived back at Palermo three days later. Within a week, the King announced that he intended to create the admiral Duke of Brontë in Sicily, giving him an estate said to be worth £3,000 a year. On the same day, Nelson transferred his flag – he was now a Rear Admiral of the Red – to a transport. He had, it seemed, temporarily relinquished service afloat, and he did not rehoist his flag in the *Foudroyant* until October.

On 5 October, he sailed for Port Mahon, Minorca, which was then in British occupation, but it was a cursory visit. He reached the island on 13 October, found affairs well conducted, stayed five days, and sped back to Palermo, where he spent the remainder of the year. His fellow officers, Troubridge and Ball in particular, grew increasingly worried at his continued residence ashore with the Hamiltons, and at the gossip which was current everywhere in the Mediterranean about what was called his 'Sicilification'.

With the new century came orders that he was to place himself under Lord Keith. The Commander-in-Chief, who had won Nelson's admiration at Toulon in 1793, when Nelson wrote of him as 'a good officer and gallant man', by this time thought coldly of Nelson, to whom he was considerably senior. Nelson joined Keith in Leghorn Roads on 25 January in the *Foudroyant*, and returned with him to Palermo, where Keith soon saw the trend of affairs. Keith's business, among other things, was to enquire why the blockade of Malta, where the French garrison under General Vaubois was holding out, was proving ineffective, and to inform himself of the state of affairs in Egypt and Syria. There, the French army's setbacks had included a repulse from Acre by the Turks (whose suzerainty extended over the entire area), assisted by ships and artillery used to great effect by Sir Sidney Smith. They were soon to surrender to forces commanded by Keith, and, on land, Abercromby.

Humiliated as he was by the presence of a superior officer in a part of the world where he was looked up to as a blend of Protector, Patron Saint, and Naval Hero, Nelson scored a professional success in Sicilian waters which gave him special pleasure. Off Cape

OPPOSITE Nelson had his detractors as well as his admirers. This Gillray cartoon gives the impression of a battered ham actor on a provincial stage rather than the hero on his quarter deck.

The HERO of the NILE.

PALMAM QUI MERUIT FERAT.

ABOVE Merton, near
Wimbledon, the estate which
Nelson bought for the
Hamiltons before his
daughter Horatia (*left*)
was born.

Passaro the squadron under his immediate orders, consisting of the *Foudroyant, Northumberland, Audacious* and the frigate *Success*, came upon a French detachment commanded by Rear Admiral Pérée, whose flag flew in the *Généreux*. This was the ship above all others that Nelson would have wished to capture, and the result was never in doubt. The British were in superior force, and Pérée surrendered. The action took place on 18 February. Just over a month later, by which time Nelson had returned to the shore, Sir Edward Berry, who had resumed his place as flag-captain, captured the *Guillaume Tell*, with the active help of the *Lion* and the frigate *Penelope*. The taking of this ship accounted for the entire French line at the battle of the Nile.

Yet, Malta still held out, and, in the erroneous belief that if he took charge of the blockade in person, Vaubois would surrender, Nelson sailed from Palermo in the *Foudroyant* on 24 April with the Hamiltons as his guests. Sir William had not been under fire since he was in the army as a young man, and he wanted to smell powder once again. Emma went because she liked adventure and wanted to be with Nelson. Vaubois supplied the cannonading for Sir William's benefit, but the French proved able to hold out for many more months.

The *Foudroyant* returned to Sicily having merely 'shown the flag'. Nelson, who was at last preparing to go home, acquired one final honour from King Ferdinand. This was the Grand Cross of the Order of St Ferdinand and Merit. He already wore the Order of the Crescent given to him by the Sultan of Turkey, in addition to his Star of the Bath. The austere Sir John Moore, who had a glimpse of Nelson at this stage of his life, described him as 'covered with stars, ribbons and medals, more like a Prince in an opera than the Conqueror of the Nile'.

Sir William Hamilton had been relieved as Minister at the Court of Naples, and as the Queen proposed to visit her mother in Vienna, Nelson took the whole party to Leghorn in the *Foudroyant*. Thence his progress home was by way of Florence, Ancona, Trieste (which he reached on board a Russian frigate), Vienna, Prague, Magdeburg and Hamburg. He was fêted everywhere, particularly in Vienna, where he sat to various artists, as did Emma. Sir William hoped that when he reached England his wife would be received at Court, and Emma extracted a letter from Maria Carolina which she hoped to present in person.

Matters turned out very differently. Gossip and scandal had preceded the party, and there was reason enough behind it, for

OPPOSITE A portrait of
Nelson by Füger, painted
during his continental
journey with the Hamiltons.

Emma was carrying Nelson's child. Fanny found the state of
affairs intolerable, and a marriage which, until Nelson's departure
from England in 1798, had been happy, was in ruins. Fanny had
nothing whatever for which to reproach herself, and the way in
which Nelson's family reorientated themselves to meet new
circumstances did them little credit.

Emma was not received at Court, as anyone could have predicted.
Nelson himself, when he attended a levée in company with his
old friend, Prince William Henry, now Duke of Clarence, and
Sir William Hamilton, made the crass mistake of appearing with
all his foreign decorations, which he had not yet had formal
permission from his own Sovereign to wear. He could scarcely
have been surprised that George III, after greeting him perfunc-
torily and enquiring whether he had recovered his health, turned
to an undistinguished general without even waiting for an
answer and talked to him with great animation.

Nelson was acting stupidly: even so, the Admiralty could not
afford to waste his professional talents, and did not intend to do
so. He had landed at Great Yarmouth on 6 November. On New
Year's Day, 1801, his name appeared in a general promotion of
flag officers in the rank of Vice Admiral of the Blue, and he was
ordered to hoist his flag on board the *San Josef* at Plymouth. This
was one of the ships he had captured on Valentine's Day, and as
Lord St Vincent was then in charge of the Channel Fleet, and once
more his Commander-in-Chief, it was as neat a way as could have
been contrived of putting Nelson back into the line of duty.

RIGHT The order of
St Ferdinand, one of the
three foreign decorations
awarded to Nelson, to the
resentment of some at
the English court.

6
The Chill of
the Baltic

At the time Nelson joined the *San Josef* he was distracted. The ship had not completed a refit, and was uncomfortable; both his eyes were giving him pain; his belongings were in disorder, for which he blamed poor Fanny, from whom he had now parted, never to see again; and he feared, misguidedly, that the Prince of Wales, to whom Sir William Hamilton was making up, would have designs on Emma.

St Vincent remarked about Nelson, with his usual acumen: 'Poor man! he is devoured with vanity, weakness and folly; was strung with ribbons, medals etc., and yet pretended he wished to avoid the honour and ceremonies he met with everywhere upon the road.' The Commander-in-Chief was at Torr Abbey; Nelson had made a call on him on his way to join his ship. St Vincent was in fact about to succeed Lord Spencer at the Admiralty, where he and Troubridge, who had become a junior member of the Board, were soon to receive reports of a very different Nelson. Whatever his private troubles, and they were manifold, nothing could alter his eminence in the sea profession.

Nelson had more or less foresworn society, but one contact he did resume; it was with his old friend Collingwood, who was also based on Plymouth. They met at the end of January, and found such pleasure in one another's company that Collingwood wrote that Nelson would probably come and live with him when the weather allowed, 'but,' he added, 'he does not get in and out of ships easily with one arm'. One evening, when the pair were dining together ashore, Collingwood's wife arrived from Northumberland with her little girl, Sarah, for a brief reunion with her husband. She was a plain woman, but good, like Fanny. Collingwood wrote to Mrs Moutray, once of Antigua, with whom he had kept up: 'How surprised you would have been to have popped in to the Fountain Inn and seen Lord Nelson, my wife, and myself sitting by the fireside cosing, and little Sarah teaching Phillis, her dog, to dance.'

Sterner occupations now awaited Nelson, who heard early in February that he was to be sent to the Baltic as second in command of a fleet entrusted to Sir Hyde Parker. His flag was transferred from the *San Josef* to the *St George*, in which he sailed for Spithead. He snatched a brief leave in London, where Emma was able to show him their new-born child, Horatia. Then he sailed for Great Yarmouth, where Parker's fleet was gathering. It had an important, intricate and dangerous mission to carry out, and much would depend on leadership.

PREVIOUS PAGES
The *Elephant* and the
British fleet sail into action
at the battle of Copenhagen.

126

Britain's communication with the Baltic countries, always important in the era of the sailing navy, had become increasingly vital, for the Baltic was the nearest and best source of essential naval stores, hemp, flax, tar, timber and copper among them. In large-scale war neutrals grow rich, but their sea-borne traffic is liable to be searched and interfered with. So acutely had this been the case during the War of American Independence that in 1780 an Armed Neutrality of the North had been formed by Russia, Denmark (whose territory then included Norway) and Sweden, to try to ensure that, suitably convoyed, their ships might trade safely even along belligerent coasts. It was also affirmed that a blockade, to be respected, must be efficient. This had not been so during the days of Britain's adversity at sea, when France and Spain had joined forces in support of the American Colonists.

By the year 1800 matters had gone so consistently badly for what was known as the Second Coalition against France, the principal members of which had been Britain, Austria and Russia, that Russia, under Tsar Paul I, actually defected. The immediate cause of Paul's dissatisfaction was his exclusion from Malta, an island upon which one of his many ambitions centred, since he had assumed 'protection' of the Knights of St John, who had been evicted by the French expedition. Malta had at last surrendered, but it was Captain Alexander Ball, not Tsar Paul I, who took control there.

One of the Tsar's reactions was to revive the idea of an Armed Neutrality, this time including Prussia in addition to Denmark and Sweden. He also showed himself wide open to diplomatic overtures from Paris. By the early months of 1801 the threat to British interests in the north was so serious that Pitt decided to intimidate the Northern Powers. If, as seemed likely, Paul was about to become at best an ill-intentioned neutral and at worst an active enemy, it was essential that he should not bring the resources of Sweden and Denmark to his support, thus adding immeasurably to the available strength at sea opposed to Britain.

The British prime minister had every justification for initiative. Britain was engaged in a life-and-death struggle, and with the Mediterranean restored to her control the Baltic area could not be allowed to fall within the enemy sphere of influence, and thus act as a counter-weight. Where the Board of Admiralty was unwise was in its choice of commander. Parker was rich, newly married, and lacked experience of high command in critical situations. Nelson was his second, to give the expedition drive.

OVERLEAF The blockade of Malta: the British fleet bombards the French occupying forces.

Sir Hyde Parker, whose limitations were highlighted by Nelson's brilliance at Copenhagen. Nelson replaced him as commander-in-chief shortly after the battle.

Unfortunately, there was no trust between Parker and Nelson, and at first very little communication. So much was this so that Nelson actually had to write privately to the Admiralty to urge haste, before Parker, suitably spurred on, would even stir from Great Yarmouth, where his wife ('batter-pudding' to the Fleet) was busy arranging a ball. When he at last arrived in northern waters, he appeared to have no considered plan of campaign, or to have decided whether Copenhagen, where the Danish fleet was known to be preparing, should be approached by way of Belt or Sound.

Once a Council of War had been assembled, Nelson's very presence and vigour charged Parker with a certain momentum. Nelson's view of Councils of War was notorious, for, as he remarked, 'If a man consults whether he is to fight, when he has the power in his own hands, *it is certain his opinion is against fighting*.' [The italics are his.]

The decision arrived at was to proceed by way of the Sound, past the castle of Kronborg, which guards one of the great sea passages of Europe. By so doing, it would be made plain from the reaction of the Governor just how sensitive Danish reaction to threat was likely to be. It would also help to clarify the attitude of Sweden, which was in possession of the opposite shore, where batteries were known to be mounted.

The orders of the Governor of Kronborg were clear. He was to resist Parker's entry into the Baltic. Bronze cannon thundered from those battlements which figure in the opening scenes in *Hamlet*, but, as Nelson noted, 'more powder and shot, I believe, never was thrown away'. Significantly, there was silence from Sweden. The sovereign of that country, Gustavus Adolphus IV, a strange unbalanced creature, had come to regard Napoleon as the Beast of the Apocalypse, and he was taking no immediate measures to antagonize Britain.

As the Kronborg firing had made it plain that the Danes, if not the Swedes, would fight, it was no surprise when Nicholas Vansittart, the Foreign Office representative who had been sent ahead to the Danish capital, notified Parker of the defiant answer he had received to the demand that Denmark should cease to take part in the Armed Neutrality. If, therefore, his own mission was not to fail, Parker would have to use force, and the sooner the better. The age abounded in instances – particularly on the French side – of threat being followed by action, without any of the niceties of diplomatic warning followed by a formal declaration of war. Parker may have hoped that threat would be enough. Nelson knew better.

... the more I have reflected [he wrote], the more I am confirmed in opinion that not a moment should be lost in attacking the enemy: they will every day and hour be stronger, we never shall be so good a match for them as at this moment. The only consideration in my mind is how to get at them with the least risk to our Ships ... I am of opinion the boldest measures are the safest, and our Country demands a most vigorous exertion of her force, directed with judgement. In supporting you, my

131

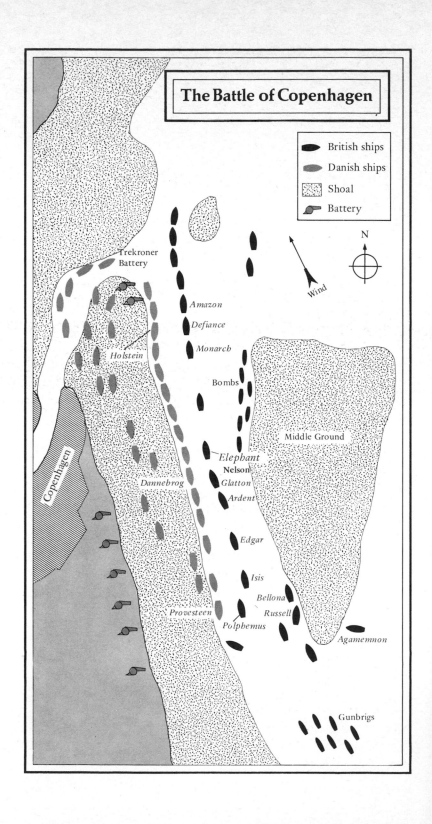

The Battle of Copenhagen

British ships
Danish ships
Shoal
Battery

N

Wind

Trekroner
Battery

Amazon

Defiance

Monarch

Holstein

Bombs

Middle Ground

Elephant
Nelson
Glatton
Ardent

Dannebrog

Edgar

Copenhagen

Isis

Bellona
Russell

Provesteen

Polphemus

Agamemnon

Gunbrigs

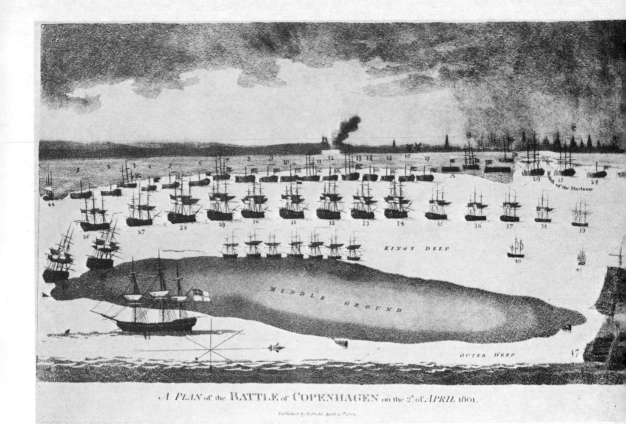

A PLAN of the BATTLE of COPENHAGEN on the 2.ᵈ of APRIL 1801.

Published by E.Pinkl April 30.ᵗʰ 1801.

dear Sir Hyde, through the arduous and important task you have undertaken, no exertion of head or heart shall be wanting from your most obedient and faithful servant NELSON AND BRONTË.

Having passed Kronborg without loss, it now remained for Parker to attack and immobilize the Danish fleet before considering further action, particularly against Russia, the main-spring of the maritime coalition. The Danes had been given ample time to prepare their defences, backed as these would be by the resources of one of the best equipped dockyards in the world, and Parker now made a sensible decision. He would entrust the fighting to Nelson! The operation would involve taking 74-gun ships, and others of lesser draught, up the intricate Kings Channel, where they would have to anchor in succession to face the line of ships and floating batteries which the Danes had made ready. Parker, with those larger vessels which could not be used in shoal water, would watch the exits from the inner harbour, from which a sortie by a Danish squadron was possible. In view of Parker's great

ABOVE A contemporary plan of the disposition of the British and Danish fleets: the Danes are at anchor in the background, guarding the entrance to Copenhagen harbour.

133

superiority in gunfire, any such move was unlikely, but at least the three-deckers would not be idle while Nelson was doing what he described as the 'warm work'.

Little went according to plan. In the early morning of 2 April, the day of the attack, the pilots attached to Nelson's squadron, faced with difficult local conditions, for the most part refused to act or gave wrong advice, and in some cases captains had to conn their ships in person. No less than three of the larger vessels grounded, the *Agamemnon*, Nelson's beloved old ship, the *Russell* and the *Bellona*. The *Agamemnon* got into trouble even before she reached the Kings Channel so that her guns were useless. The others took at least some part in the battle, and in fact it was through Robert Southey's brother, Tom, who was a lieutenant on board the *Bellona*, that a series of details were supplied for the most popular of all lives of Nelson.

When the two sides were ranged parallel, fire soon became tremendous. The Danes were well supplied with powder and shot, they were defending their own territory, and they were under the eye of their Prince Royal, who was the effective ruler of the kingdom. Among the ships engaged most hotly were the British frigates, who found themselves exposed to the fire of the Trekroner battery near the heavily defended harbour entrance.

Throughout the engagement, there was close-range fire of the most punishing kind, with no opportunity for manœuvring or finesse. The Danes were moored. Nelson's larger ships were anchored by the bows, as had been the case at the Nile, with springs on the cables which allowed captains some limited freedom of movement. But in general, and throughout, the battle was an exhausting, almost static duel in which the side which loaded fastest and aimed straightest had every advantage. Experience told heavily, and so did training. The Danes were short of trained gunners. The British had years of hard fighting behind them, as well as a tradition of victory.

After a few hours of what must have seemed to him agonizing uncertainty, Parker, four miles or so away from the scene of encounter, could bear the suspense no longer. Thereupon, he made one of the most unfortunate signals ever recorded. He ordered Nelson to discontinue fighting, and this at the very crisis of the battle when, as it happened, Danish resistance was slackening. Nelson's reaction, though well known, bears telling once again as exemplifying the character of a great commander, not afraid to disobey orders when he knows he is right in so doing. The

134

account comes from an eye-witness, Colonel Stewart, who was in charge of the troops serving on board the *Elephant*, which flew Nelson's flag at the time of the battle. He saw what happened a few minutes later:

... Nelson now walked the deck considerably agitated, which was always known by his moving the stump of his right arm. After a turn or two, he said to me in a quick manner: 'Do you know what's shown on board of the Commander-in-Chief – No. 39.' On asking him what that meant he answered: 'Why, to leave off Action.' 'Leave off action!' he repeated, and then added, with a shrug, 'Now, damn me if I do.' He also observed, I believe, to Captain Foley: 'You know, Foley, I have only one eye. I have a right to be blind sometimes', and then, with an archness peculiar to his character, putting the glass to his blind eye, he exclaimed: 'I really do not see the Signal!' This remarkable Signal was, therefore, only acknowledged on board the *Elephant*, not repeated.

The signal resulted in at least one shocking loss. Captain Riou, in the frigate *Amazon*, who was one of the finest of all Parker's subordinates, saw it and obeyed, and was killed in the act of turning his ship out of the direct line of fire. Even had Nelson's other captains followed Riou's move, they could scarcely have done so with impunity, so critical was their position between a shoal and an enemy still very active.

Shortly after this incident, Nelson sent a missive ashore. It was carefully composed, and even more carefully sealed, so that it should not appear to have been despatched in haste. The wording and arrangement, which is here taken from the original, preserved in Denmark, is generally transcribed from Nelson's letter-book. There, the wording does not always follow the original.

Lord Nelson has directions to spare Denmark, when no longer resisting but if the firing is continued on the part of Denmark, Lord Nelson will be obliged to set on fire all the floating batteries he has taken, without having the power of saving the Brave Danes who have defended them.

> Dated on board His Britannick
> Majestys Ship *Elephant*
> Copenhagen Roads April 2nd 1801
>
> *Nelson & Brontë, Vice*
> *Admiral under the Command of Admiral Sir Hyde Parker*

To the Brothers of Englishmen
The Danes.

Firing ceased altogether when Lindholm, the Danish Adjutant-General, came on board Nelson's ship under a flag of truce, but

The British fleet bombards
the Danes. The bulbous
towers of Copenhagen are
visible through the smoke,
behind the Danish ships.

136

Nelson's task was by no means over. He had to extricate his squadron, three vessels still grounded, and all the rest damaged. He had to make arrangements about the prizes. He had to rendezvous with and report to Parker, and he soon perceived it was likely to fall to him rather than to Parker to arrange the terms of an Armistice. Weary as he was, action had toned him up, as it always did, and having achieved a tactical victory, now was the time to follow it up.

It was this gathering of the fruits of battle that Nelson knew to be the acid test. He had failed at Naples. Now he had been given another chance. Copenhagen had been costly in life and limb: the sacrifice must not be wasted. The actual figures of loss now generally accepted were, on the British side, 253 killed and 688 wounded, and on the Danish, 790 killed and 910 wounded. As was always his way, one of Nelson's main cares was for the wounded, who included Captain Thompson of the *Bellona*, one of his Nile 'Band of Brothers'. Thompson had lost a leg, and was in great pain. Captain Mosse of the *Monarch*, which had suffered more than any other ship of the line, had been among the killed. The list also included Captain Bawden, a Rifleman who had been serving in the *Elephant* under Colonel Stewart.

By one of those tragic ironies commonplace in history, an event had occurred in the Russian capital, over a week before, which, had its longer-term effects been known, would have rendered all fighting unnecessary. Tsar Paul, who had become increasingly unbalanced and at times frenzied, had been murdered in his palace at St Petersburg by members of his entourage. Even when the news spread, it was at first uncertain whether his son and successor, Alexander I, would adhere to his father's foreign policy.

In the meanwhile, there was a convention to be agreed with the Danish Prince Royal before the British fleet could proceed eastwards into Swedish and Russian waters, to concert the next steps. Nelson landed in Copenhagen with powers from Parker to negotiate. There he had a long interview with the august personage who was later to reign as Frederik VI. The negotiations, an account of which Nelson sent direct to Downing Street, were in English, the only language of which Nelson had command. Fortunately the Prince Royal was also at ease in it, which was not unnatural since he had an English mother and grandmother, his mother being a sister of George III.

There are conflicting accounts of Nelson's reception, a Danish authority stating that he was met 'as one brave enemy ought ever

OPPOSITE It was Tsar Paul's foreign policy which precipitated the war with Denmark. He was succeeded a week before Copenhagen by his son, Alexander I (*opposite*), who reversed his policies, and sent a conciliatory message to Nelson after the battle.

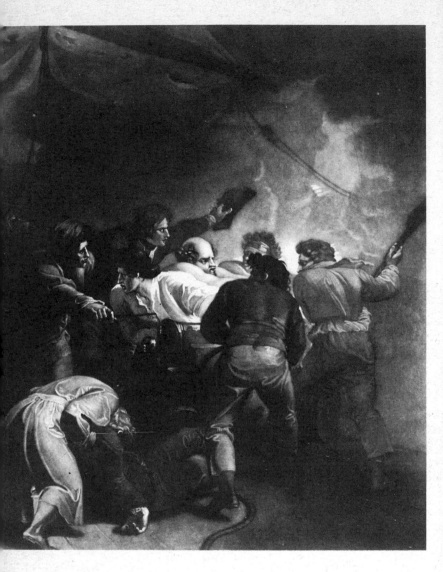

Sailors in a Fight by Stothard, 1798.
ABOVE The gun crew were not only in danger
from the enemy: the massive guns
recoiled on firing and sometimes broke
from their moorings, causing injury
and adding to the confusion of battle.
RIGHT A sailor hacks at the rigging
to prevent boarding from an enemy ship
drawing alongside.

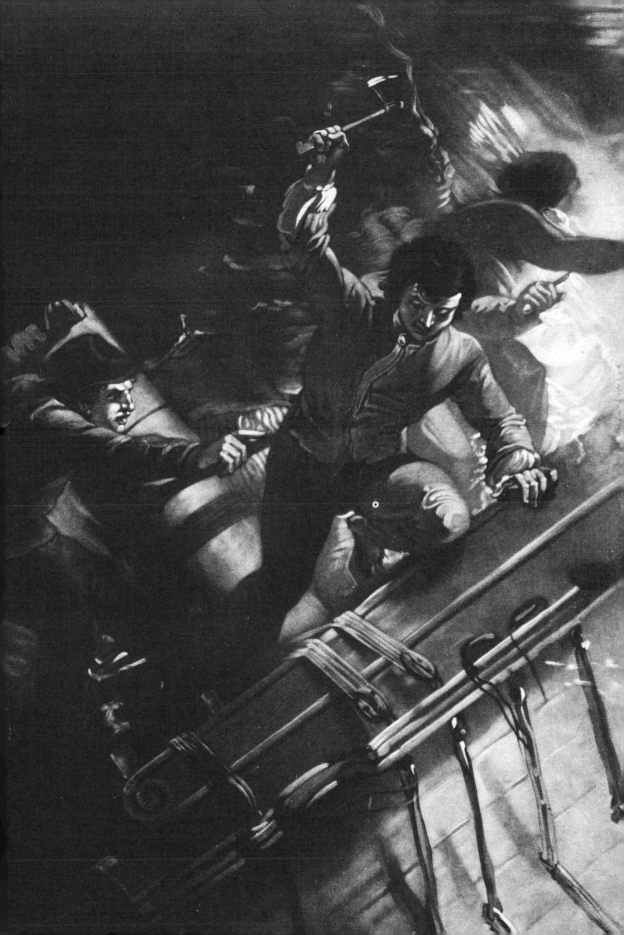

to receive another – with respect. A carriage was provided for his lordship, which, however, he declined, and he walked amidst an immense crowd of persons, anxious to catch a glimpse of the hero, to the Palace of the Prince.' Colonel Stewart remarked that 'the populace showed a mixture of admiration, curiosity and displeasure'. It would scarcely have been in human nature, considering the length of the Danish casualty list, if displeasure had not been an active ingredient; but Nelson intended to show the same courage in the midst of a partly hostile crowd as he had always done in the face of enemy fire.

Admiral and Prince were together for two hours, alone except for Adjutant-General Lindholm; no Ministers were about, since the talk was to be informal and 'exploratory'. Nelson asked if he might speak his mind openly. The Prince welcomed such freedom, and after ranging round the subject of neutral trade in time of war, the Prince suddenly came to the question he must have been burning to ask from the outset.

'Pray answer me,' he said to Nelson, 'for what is the British Fleet come into the Baltic?' Nelson replied: 'To crush a most formidable and unprovoked coalition against Great Britain . . .'. The Prince said that this was a misunderstanding, and that his uncle, George III, had been deceived, 'and that nothing should ever make him take a part against Great Britain, for that it could not be to his interest to see us crushed, nor, he trusted, ours to see him,' to which Nelson agreed. Nelson then said: 'there could not be a doubt of the hostility of Denmark, for if her fleet had been joined with Russia and Sweden, they would assuredly have gone into the North Sea, menaced the coast of England, and probably have joined the French, had they been able.' The Prince said that his ships should never join any Power against England, 'but,' said Nelson, 'it required not much argument to satisfy him that he could not help it.'

After some further general remarks, the Prince asked what immediate conditions would satisfy the British. Nelson could not say with any precision, but the Prince pressed him for his personal opinion.

'First', he said, 'a free entry of the British Fleet into Copenhagen, and the free use of everything we may want from it.' Before he could continue, the Prince said quickly: 'That you should have with pleasure.' 'The next,' said Nelson, 'while this explanation (negotiation) is going on, a total suspension of your treaties with Russia. These, I believe, are the foundation on which Sir Hyde Parker only can build other articles for his justification in suspending his orders, which are plain and positive.'

The Prince then asked his visitor to recapitulate what he had

142

said, and thanked him for his 'open conversation'. Both men then apologized for anything they might have said which had been too warmly expressed, Nelson concluding that his whole reception 'was such as I have always found it, far beyond my deserts'.

A few days later Nelson paid a second visit to the city. Colonel Stewart, who was present on this occasion, noted that the crowd 'showed more satisfaction than on the preceding one'. This was not surprising, since the results of the battle were by that time less visibly in evidence. Parker now entrusted Nelson with formal

No medals were struck after the battle, but unofficial badges were presented to some of those who fought at Copenhagen.

143

powers of negotiation, and the most difficult subject proved to be the duration of the armistice, which the British wished to be for sixteen weeks, Nelson assuring the Danes, with a degree of candour not quite usual in diplomacy, that the reason for requiring so long a term was that they might have time to act against the Russians, and then return.

The point not being acceded to on either side [reported Stewart], one of the Danish Commissioners hinted at a renewal of hostilities. Upon which Lord Nelson, who understood French sufficiently well to make out what the Commissioner said (for the parley was conducted in this tongue), turned to one of his friends with warmth, and said: 'Renew hostilities! Tell him we are ready in a moment: ready to bombard this very night.' The Commissioner apologised with politeness, and the business went on more amicably. The duration of the armistice could not, however, be adjusted, and the conference broke up for reference to the Prince.

While the Danes were considering, a reception was held in one of the State Rooms, the whole of which were without furniture, from apprehension of the very threat which Nelson had just uttered. Later, Nelson proceeded upstairs to a grand dinner, the Prince leading the way. The admiral, leaning on the arm of a friend, whispered, 'Though I have only one eye, I see all this will burn very well.'

In the end, fourteen weeks of armistice was agreed to, the other principal terms stipulating that the Armed Neutrality should be suspended on the part of Denmark, that Copenhagen should be unmolested, that the British should be free to purchase provisions in Denmark, and that the local coasting trade should be safeguarded. The appropriate document was duly ratified by the Prince and by Parker, and then Colonel Stewart was despatched to England. He went as official messenger, and as an unofficial public relations officer for Nelson.

The admiral liked to distribute mementoes of his visits, and Copenhagen received more than one. A day or so after the conference he sent ashore to Captain Sneedorff, who was then at the head of the Naval Academy, one of the gold medals which his prize agent, Alexander Davison, had struck in commemoration of the battle of the Nile. The letter which accompanied it concluded as follows:

I send you also a short account of my life, it cannot do harm to youth and may do good, as it will show that perseverance and good conduct will raise a person to the very highest honours and rewards. That it may be useful in that way to those entrusted to your care is the fervent wish of your most obedient servant, NELSON AND BRONTË.

It is scarcely surprising, in view of such sublime assurance first in battle and later in negotiation, that one of the results of Stewart's mission was the instant supercession of Sir Hyde Parker, and his replacement by Nelson as Commander-in-Chief. Nelson was sorry at the way that Admiralty saw fit to recall Parker so summarily, but at least it meant that he could now order measures with despatch. Nelson was anxious to finish this northern business, and to go home. There had been some talk of an enquiry about the whole conduct of affairs in the Baltic. Nelson wrote privately that Parker's real friends would never wish for this to take place. He added:

His friends in the Fleet wish everything of this Fleet to be forgot, for we all respect and love Sir Hyde; but the dearer his friends, the more uneasy they have been at his *idleness*, for that is the truth – no criminality. I believe Sir H. P. to be as good a subject as his Majesty has.

With the unconscious arrogance typical of him, Nelson sent to one of the defeated Danes a Nile Medal and an account of his life, together with a letter pointing out the virtue of emulating his example.

145

By 'criminality' Nelson meant personal hanging back, or what Lord Howe and earlier admirals used to describe as 'shyness'. Yet idleness in crisis, and nervelessness in battle deserve hard words. Collingwood, who was as shrewd a judge of men as anyone living, wrote of Parker in harsher terms than had Nelson.

I cannot but wonder the Admiralty should be so anxious to have him employed, for in the little I have seen of him I could only discover a good tempered man, full of vanity, a great deal of pomp, and a pretty smattering of ignorance – nothing of that natural ability that raises men without the advantage of a learned education.

With Nelson in full charge, everything was transformed. His first signal was for the fleet to prepare to weigh anchor.

This [wrote Stewart], at once showed how different a system was about to be pursued, it having been intended that the Fleet should await at anchor fresh instructions from England relative to the state of Northern affairs.

Lord Nelson, who foresaw every bad consequence from this inactive mode of proceeding, owed his bad health to chagrin more than to any other cause. The joy with which the signal was received not only manifested what are the customary feelings on those occasions, but was intended as peculiarly complimentary to the admiral.

On 7 May the Fleet left Kioge Bay, and proceeding towards Bornholm, anchored, in blowing weather, off that island. The greater part was here left to watch the motions of the Swedes; and with a chosen squadron, consisting of his best-sailing 74's, two frigates, a brig and a schooner, Lord Nelson sailed for the Port of Revel. He wished for further satisfaction respecting the friendly disposition of the Russians, and thought that the best method of putting this to the proof would be to try how he should be received in one of their Ports. He sincerely desired peace, but had no apprehension of hostilities.

Parker had already sent his old friend Captain Fremantle on a mission to St Petersburg, where he was well received, and where he heard something of the character of the former Tsar which made him 'surprised to think he was suffered to live so long'. It was soon clear that no mischief was to be expected either from Russia or from Sweden. Gustavus Adolphus IV ordered his ships to remain within Karlscrona, and a little later came news that British merchant seamen who had been detained in Russian ports were to be released. Nelson's task was done, and he was allowed to return to England, fortified by a letter from the First Lord of the Admiralty which would have warmed anyone's heart.

I never saw the man in our Profession [wrote the Earl of St Vincent], excepting yourself and Troubridge, who possessed the magic art of infusing the same spirit into others, which inspired their own actions, exclusive of other talents and habits of business not common to naval characters. . . . Your Lordship's whole conduct, from your first appointment to this hour, is the subject of our constant admiration. It does not become me to make comparisons: all agree there is but one Nelson. That he may long continue the pride of his Country is the fervent wish of your Lordship's truly affectionate ST VINCENT.

Nelson was given a step in the peerage for his feat in battle and his skill in negotiation, and his tactical second, Rear Admiral Graves, was knighted. But Nelson was mortified because no recognition, in the form of gold medals such as had been bestowed after other outstanding successes by the Fleet, was given to captains who had distinguished themselves in the Baltic. There were two reasons for this. The first was because Britain and Denmark were not formally at war. The second was that it would have been preposterous to have decorated Parker, or the captains of the larger but disengaged ships of the line. Yet the matter rankled with Nelson for the rest of his life: he felt fiercely indignant that his captains should not have had their due.

Although, technically, the British moves had been 'preventative', Nelson actually left the Baltic convinced that, sooner or later, there would be renewed trouble, not least with Denmark. He was right, though he did not live to see that particular phase of the long drawn out struggle.

Even in earlier days as a captain on convoy duty, Nelson had never cared for the chill of the Baltic, and he was thankful when the Admiralty sent out a replacement. Nelson sailed home in a brig, and, for the second time within a year, landed at Great Yarmouth. There he visited wounded men from his command who were still in the local hospital. Then he sped to London. He was allowed a brief leave, which he spent with the Hamiltons, who were on a fishing holiday.

On 24 July he was appointed Commander-in-Chief of a force employed between Orfordness and Beachy Head to prevent invasion. Bonaparte had his Grand Army arrayed on the French coast of the Channel, flotillas prepared for the day when he judged conditions to be favourable for troops to embark. The threat was taken seriously, whatever later historians say. Sea Fencibles, a kind of maritime Home Guard, had been organized, and people in general felt safer when Vice Admiral Viscount Nelson KB was there.

China made in commemoration of the Baltic campaign. The plate opposite is a contemporary Chinese copy of a dinner service made for the Nelson family. The '22' instead of '2 April' (the actual date of the battle of Copenhagen) establishes it as a fake.

Like Drake before him, Nelson believed in a 'home stroke'. Britain should not await invasion passively, or even depend on her main fleet, but should attack the enemy in his own harbours. The one chosen was Boulogne, which was attacked in force on the night of 18 August. Nelson did not take part in person, but his orders were characteristic:

When any boats have taken one vessel, the business is not to be considered as finished, but a sufficient number being left to guard the prize, the others are immediately to pursue the object by proceeding to the next, and so on until the whole of the Flotilla be either taken or totally annihilated, for there must not be the smallest cessation until their destruction is completely finished.... Watchword, *Nelson*: the answer, *Brontë*.

The French were well prepared, and the attack was a costly failure, with many casualties. St Vincent, who had approved the operation, was as generous about it as he had been about Teneriffe. Nelson had completely redeemed himself in his chief's eyes by his conduct in the Baltic, and St Vincent now believed him fit for the highest responsibilities, however much he might deplore his private life.

By now, the war had reached a stage of stalemate when a pause, or even a Peace of sorts, seemed probable. On land everything, except in Egypt, the West Indies and the Far East, had gone the French way. By sea, Britain held supremacy. Pitt was temporarily out of office, living at Walmer Castle as Warden of the Cinque Ports. There Nelson visited him, for they were friends, and were much the same age. Addington was now Prime Minister, and it was to him that Nelson had reported his conversations with the Danish Prince Royal.

149

The Government was so actively engaged in negotiations with France that some of the mobilized forces were stood down. In October 1801, Nelson was allowed indefinite leave of absence. He took the Portsmouth Road towards London, turning aside at Merton, near Wimbledon, where he had recently acquired a handsome property, to which he hoped to add. There he proposed to live with the Hamiltons, and there he could receive his relations, including his little daughter, who was considered as being

To forestall an invasion of
England, the British fleet
unsuccessfully attacked
Boulogne. The French sail
from the harbour to
meet them.

'adopted'. Only Fanny and Josiah felt the cold, for eventually even
Edmund Nelson, to whom Fanny had always been so attentive,
and who had always considered himself free to reside for much of
each year away from Burnham Thorpe, paid one visit, shortly
before his death at Bath. He acknowledged, somewhat wryly, that
his famous son seemed happy, even if his favourite daughter-in-
law was not. Emma saw to that, and her campaign of vilification
continued until she infected the entire Nelson family.

151

Between voyages Nelson returned
to Merton (*above*), where Emma
(*right*) held her own court, being
excluded from the place she had
hoped to occupy in polite society.
She is framed by the candelabra at
the card party on the far right, one
of the few representations of her
which show her heavy build.
All these drawings are
by Thomas Baxter.

ABOVE William Hamilton bequeathed to Nelson this
miniature of Emma, a copy of an original by
Vigée le Brun. It was treasured by Nelson, and
is thought to be one of the truest likenesses.
RIGHT An unfinished portrait of Nelson by Beechey.

7 Storm-Tossed Ships

THE TIME between late October 1801 and May 1803 which Nelson spent ashore, possibly the happiest of his life, belongs to private rather than to public history. Professionally, he had fulfilled himself. He was marked for high command if and when war was resumed; and he was gratified by general recognition.

He loved Merton, did much to improve it, and was able to have friends and family about him as he wished. Fanny moved from lodging to lodging, sustained by a quarterly allowance from her husband of £400. Josiah found other directions than the Navy for such ability as he possessed. Later on in life, his energy was given to money-making, for which he had some aptitude. Both people who had loomed large in Nelson's earlier spell ashore were now dismissed from his life. The distance between 1792 and 1801 was, in a domestic way, unbridgeable.

Emma presided at Merton, though the place was Nelson's. Sir William Hamilton had taken a house in Piccadilly, so that Nelson, in effect, had two homes, both highly convenient. He even began to share some of Sir William's cultivated tastes, though Merton itself was too like a Nelson Museum to please the more fastidious.

In July and August 1802 he made an extended tour with the Hamiltons which included Oxford, Birmingham and a visit to Sir William's estate in the district of Milford Haven. This became a triumphal progress. People turned out in crowds to welcome the one-armed hero, who so clearly enjoyed applause. His passion for Emma was unabated, and the pleasure he took in Horatia was such that, had he been longer ashore, he would have become a possessive parent, even if an unacknowledged one.

When winter came, Sir William began to suffer in health. The damp climate of England did not suit him after so many sunny years in Italy. He had sold most of his artistic collections, and during his last years seemed to take more pleasure in fishing than in other occupations. His homes were apt to be tempestuous. Emma, given her head, was extravagant, noisy and fond of strong drink. She was not received in quarters where Fanny found a welcome. This saddened her patient husband, and when, early in 1803, he felt that his illness had become grave, he removed to Piccadilly, so that Merton should have no associations with unhappiness. He died in London on 6 April 1803, watched over by his wife and friend.

A sentence in his will expressed his view of Nelson, to whom he left a copy of Vigée le Brun's portrait of Emma, the original of which he had disposed of, much to Nelson's annoyance:

Sir William, *cognoscente*, loving husband and kind friend – to the acid pen of Gillray (*opposite*), an eccentric and deluded cuckold.

... the copy ... in enamel by Bone, I give to my dearest friend Lord Nelson Duke of Brontë, a very small token of the great regard I have for his lordship, the most virtuous, loyal and truly brave character I ever met with. God bless him, and shame fall on those who do not say amen.

There was nothing equivocal about that: and as a further memento he left Nelson two guns. In view of the state of Europe at the time, nothing could have been more appropriate.

It came about that by the early summer of 1803, Bonaparte was ready to resume war with England. Shortly after an outburst to the British ambassador which, years later, he said he regretted, he

160

A COGNOCENTI contemplating y^e Beauties of y^e Antique.

committed an act as unforgivable as anything in his career. English civilians had flocked to France during the interlude of peace, renewing contact with what they had supposed was civilization. Bonaparte detained them, 10,000 in all, and they were prisoners for eleven years. There was an added bitterness in Nelson's allusions to the French after the year 1803, in which he was echoed by most of his contemporaries. Bonaparte held a grubby trump card, since there were few Frenchmen in England who could be detained in reciprocation. He did not scruple to play it.

Britain should by this time have been very strongly equipped at sea, but she was handicapped by the policy followed by St Vincent during his regime at the Admiralty, which lasted from February 1801 to November 1803. Determined to root out corruption in the dockyards, he brought work there almost to a standstill. That was why when, on 16 May 1803, Nelson was appointed to be Commander-in-Chief, Mediterranean, with the duty of watching Toulon, he had to make do, for many months, with few ships, and fewer supplies. He had many problems. Not the least of them was to keep the sea in adequate strength.

He was given the *Victory* as his flag-ship, the splendid three-decker, laid down during the Seven Years War, which had flown St Vincent's flag on Valentine's Day, 1797, and that of many other renowned admirals. Nelson sailed in her from Spithead on 20 May. His principal fellow Commander-in-Chief was his old friend Cornwallis, who had charge of what was known as the Western Squadron or Channel Fleet. So pressed was Cornwallis for ships, that Nelson transferred to the frigate *Amphion* so that Cornwallis could have the use of the *Victory* for as long as he wished. Cornwallis did not retain the ship a day longer than necessary, and by July she arrived at Gibraltar.

The *Victory* had as her original flag-captain under Nelson's regime Samuel Sutton, an old friend who had served for many years in the Mediterranean, always with distinction. He had commanded the *Egmont* at the battle of St Vincent, and the frigate *Alcmene* at Copenhagen. In due course, he would be replaced by Hardy, with whom Nelson sailed in the *Amphion*, for Sutton was too senior not to be given a 'private' ship.

As Chief of Staff or 'First Captain', Nelson took George Murray, who was shortly due for promotion to the flag officer's list. Murray had as high a reputation as anyone of his rank in the Navy. As a young man he had served in the Far East in the fierce duels with

Suffren, during the War of American Independence. He had commanded the *Colossus* at St Vincent, and the *Edgar* at Copenhagen. Nelson knew him well and liked him greatly. With a large chin and gentle ways, Murray was much loved and respected.

He had hesitated to accept what was apt to be a difficult post. He made the point that 'the nature of the service was such, as very frequently terminated in disagreement between the admiral and the captain: and he should be extremely unwilling to hazard any possible thing that should diminish the regard and respect which he should ever entertain for his lordship'. Nelson resolved his doubts in a characteristic way. He agreed that there could be difficulties, but assured Murray that, 'on whatever service he might be called, or whatever measure he might be directed to carry into execution, he never should forget the intimacy which subsisted between them; and even, should anything go contrary to his wishes, he would waive the rank of *Admiral*, and explain, or expostulate with him as his *Friend*'. Such an appeal was irresistible. During the two years in which Nelson and Murray were together, there was no serious rift between them. Murray's promotion to Rear Admiral of the Blue was gazetted eleven months after he joined the *Victory*. In normal circumstances, he would then have left for a more senior appointment, but in fact he stayed on with Nelson until the Commander-in-Chief's return to England in 1805.

The log of the *Victory* is one of those records which have lasting interest as showing the day-to-day movements of the flag-ship of the foremost tactician of his day. But it has two sides, and one of them is dark. With Hardy as ship's captain, his role as a 'taut hand' was in no doubt. In the period when Nelson was maintaining his watch on Toulon, inspiring that much-quoted sentence of Mahan's about 'those far-distant, storm-beaten ships, upon which the Grand Army never looked', which 'stood between it and the dominion of the world', the load of physical suffering among the 'People' was terrible.

Between the end of July 1803, when the *Victory* joined the fleet in the Gulf of Lions, and December 1804, there were 380 entries relating to the infliction of the lash. In one period alone, from January to July 1804, one hundred and five men were flogged, thirteen of them more than once. An outstanding case is that of John Walsh, who was punished four times; for theft (12 lashes: 10 January); drunkenness (36 lashes: 24 March); more drunkenness (48 lashes: 5 April); and more theft (48 lashes: 24 May). So much for physical punishment as a deterrent.

Thomas Hardy was a harsh
captain, and it is clear that
Nelson must bear some of
the responsibility for
condoning his flag-captain's
fondness for the lash.

There was even an instance, during the same period, of a 'flog-ging round the fleet'. This was inflicted on Richard Collins, William Brown and John Marshall on 31 March. They were con-demned to receive 200 lashes, 50 alongside the *Victory* herself, and 50 alongside three other ships. Their crime was desertion, pre-sumably while on a watering party ashore. Desertion was punish-able by death. Whether Nelson's alternative was more merciful must be a matter of opinion. Certainly it was given as an awful example to men with similar aspirations to escape. The 'crimes' most commonly noted were 'fighting', 'uncleanness', 'insolence', 'contempt', 'theft', 'drunkenness' and 'disobedience'. Victimiza-tion of one sort or another must have been on a considerable scale.

When he was a captain, Nelson's record of punishments was not negligible, though it was never excessive, and seems to have been just, according to the ideas of the time. As an admiral, he would have supported his flag-captain's attitude towards it. There is evidence that Nelson left much to his subordinates, far more so than, for instance, Collingwood, who as a captain had punished when he felt compelled to do so, but as an admiral discouraged flogging, and saw to it that his captains acted as he wished. He sometimes referred to such officers as his 'assistants', as if he per-sonally saw to the running of everything, as indeed he did.

In respect of punishments, as in his undeviating reverence for existing Constitutions, Nelson was more of a man of his time than Collingwood, who had no use whatever, for instance, for Ferdinand of Naples and his regime. He did not even trouble to pay his respects at the Court of the Two Sicilies for some years after taking over command in the Mediterranean.

It took many decades before flogging was 'suspended' in the Navy, which, in practical terms, meant that it ceased. In 1871 it was 'suspended in peace time' and eight years later it was 'sus-pended in war time'. (It was abolished in the army in 1881.) Nelson undoubtedly inspired love, among officers and men alike, but it was in the hearts of the volunteers, who were not a high proportion of many ship's companies. The wretched pressed men had their sufferings multiplied, and Nelson, from his eminence as Com-mander-in-Chief of one of his country's principal fleets, could have thought back to his boyhood, and to his first sea voyage in a merchantman, when he learnt how the Navy was hated. The remedy only came when, in mid-nineteenth century, Impressment disappeared in favour of enlistment on proper terms.

In the light of hindsight, it is not difficult to condemn Hardy's

ABOVE The *Victory* was a distinguished
ship before she became a legendary
one. A succession of well-known officers
captained her. Here she flies
Vice-Admiral Lord Hood's flag in
the Mediterranean in 1793. Nelson was
given her as flag-ship in 1803.
Except for a brief period, Nelson sailed
in her for the rest of his life.

166

RIGHT Lord Collingwood;
Nelson's friend and
fellow officer.

HMS Victory

Today, at anchor in Portsmouth, the *Victory*'s beauty is as startling as her history is enthralling. It is easy to forget the blood that was spilled making that history: her gun decks (*below*) were painted red so the sight of their companions blood should not daunt the men in battle.

No lounge of a modern liner
could compete with the
elegance of Nelson's cabin
on the *Victory*.

The amenities of an officer's life
at sea was not shared by the men, who
lived in cramped quarters below decks, and
slept in hammocks slung between beams.

methods, and there are indications that Murray, as Captain of the Fleet, was of another way of thought. Hardy could have been overruled, and as Nelson did not do this, he bears responsibility for the ruthless severity employed in the *Victory*. A study in detail of her log and Muster Book, and a comparison with those of other ships in the Fleet, would make a valuable contribution to a fuller picture of lower-deck life in Nelson's era. John Masefield, who attempted the task, was moved to say that 'our naval glory was built up by the blood and agony of thousands of barbarously mal-treated men'.

By contrast, the life of the admiral and his immediate staff or 'Family' was one of amenities, although for nearly two years, Nelson never set foot outside his ship. For a man of his energy and vitality and range of interests, this would have been a penance at least distantly approaching that of the men he commanded. As the complexity of the war broadened, so did his problems grow. He only lived to resolve one of them, and that was the fate of the Toulon fleet.

Bonaparte had made the British retention of Malta, in spite of treaty stipulations, a *casus belli*. Geographically, the island was too far east to be of much immediate use to Nelson, who favoured the facilities offered by the Maddalena Islands, a group off the northern coast of Sardinia, as anchorage and watering place, the local water being particularly good. But as an *entrepôt* for the British trade with the Levant, Malta flourished under the governorship of Nelson's friend, Captain Ball, once of HMS *Alexander* and among the 'Band of Brothers' at the Nile.

In addition to the Captain of the Fleet and the Flag Captain, Nelson's 'Family' included the Surgeon, the Secretary, John Scott, and the 'Chaplain and Secretary for Foreign Correspondence', also named Scott, who was master of several languages. Dr Gillespie, the Surgeon, sent home a lyrical account of life during the years of blockade, but he picked a fine day for his description, not one of those which make the Gulf of Lions no place for a land lubber.

At 6 o'clock my servant brings a light, and informs me of the hour, wind, weather and course of the ship, when I immediately dress and generally repair to the deck. . . . Breakfast is announced in the Admiral's cabin . . . tea, hot rolls, cold tongue etc., which when finished we repair upon deck to enjoy the majestic sight of the rising sun (scarcely ever obscured in this fine climate). . . .

Between the hours of 7 and 2 there is plenty of time for business, study, writing and exercise. At 2 o'clock a band of music plays till within a

172

quarter of 3, when the drum beats the tune called 'The Roast Beef of Old England', to announce the Admiral's dinner, which is served up exactly at three o'clock, and which generally consists of three courses and a dessert of the choicest fruit, together with three or four of the best wines, champagne and claret not excepted ... If a person does not feel himself perfectly at ease it must be his own fault, such is the urbanity and hospitality which reign here.

Gillespie went on to describe the deck exercise which followed, accompanied by the band once again; then tea, between 6 and 7 o'clock, and conversation, Nelson 'being at all times as free from stiffness and pomp as a regard to proper dignity will admit'. At 8 o'clock there was a rummer of punch, with cake or biscuit. Soon afterwards, the 'Family' wished their chief goodnight, Nelson usually being in bed before 9 o'clock. 'Such,' concluded the Surgeon, 'is the journal of a day at sea in fine or at least moderate weather, in which this floating castle goes through the water with the greatest imaginable steadiness.'

The *Victory* was in a sense an epitome of life generally where, in words used later by Disraeli, who perceived their truth, 'I was told that the Privileged and the People formed Two Nations'. The victualling scale on which the People of the Navy worked was 1 lb of salt pork or 2 lb of beef on alternate days; a daily ration of 1 lb of biscuit (full of weevils) and a gallon of beer. This was supplemented by a weekly issue of 2 pints of pease, 3 of oatmeal, 8 oz of butter, and 1 lb of cheese. Although this was the official ration, and not an unsubstantial one, he was a lucky man who got it, even after a reduction of one-eighth which was supposed to compensate the Purser, who looked after supplies, for wastage and seepage.

In the Mediterranean the seamen drank wine, as often as not, in place of beer, which did not keep. Nelson made every use of anti-scorbutics, and in particular the lemon, which had long been known as a sovereign remedy against scurvy, though the fact was often forgotten by officialdom. Nelson had learnt the importance of such dietary precautions during the War of American Independence, when 'essence of spruce' had sometimes been resorted to. This was a preventative discovered from the Indians by the French in Canada. It had been employed by the British at the time of Wolfe's expedition to Quebec.

The officers and men of the *Victory* had been at sea for a year when, in May 1804, Bonaparte transformed himself from First Consul to Emperor of the French. As a soldier, his main concern was the Grand Army encamped on the shores of the Channel, as it had been for so long. There is still visible evidence, the remains of martello towers, military canals, and other preparations, that the threat of invasion was taken seriously by a Government once again headed by William Pitt.

Another significant event of the year 1804 was that Bonaparte persuaded Spain to renew war against Britain. Spain had never been whole-hearted in her alliances with France. Bonaparte was later to inflame Spanish national feeling by his atrocious behaviour to the Spanish Royal Family, whom he imprisoned. While Nelson lived, it cannot be said that Spain added much to such anxieties as the Navy was already enduring. It is true that it meant that there were more ships to be watched. On the other hand, there was a far better prospect of prize money. It was captures from Spain more than from France which had been the foundation of many naval fortunes.

Nelson was never tired of insisting that his ships did not sail the Gulf of Lions in order to keep the French in Toulon, but with the hope that they would come out, so that he could fight them. Admiral Latouche-Tréville, who had beaten off Nelson's light forces when they attacked Boulogne in 1801, had command of the French Mediterranean Fleet. When he died, in August 1804, he was replaced by Pierre Villeneuve, one of the few French officers who had escaped the holocaust of Aboukir Bay. Bonaparte considered Villeneuve to be 'lucky', which was why he sent him to Toulon. He was, in fact, a man of average intelligence who was scared stiff of Nelson, a characteristic which showed good sense. He was forty-one, had comparatively little battle experience and, had it not been for the Revolution, he would probably never have attained flag rank at all. He now found himself cast for the principal part in one of those majestic schemes of strategy of which his master was fond, which generally looked so well on paper.

The idea was a union of all the principal French and Spanish squadrons – from Toulon, Cartagena, Cadiz, Rochefort and Brest. They should evade the British, and sail for the West Indies. There, having disrupted the rich trade of the British-owned islands, they should take up their battle order and sweep back to Europe, a mighty Combined Fleet. Their presence in such strength would, so Bonaparte believed, cause the opposing fleet to scatter. Then it would be the turn of the invasion flotillas, packed with veteran troops, to cross to England. The sequel could safely be left to military genius – no one doubted whose. Bonaparte had no opinion of the British land forces, and indeed the British army had been

174

given no chance, as yet, to show its capacity on any extended scale since the start of the war. Its glory was all in the future, under Wellington.

Villeneuve's 'luck' held, in that he twice got away from Toulon, in January and in March 1805. Each time, watching frigates were shaken off, but in January the French met with one of those Gulf of Lions gales with which Nelson had grown so familiar, and they put back, badly damaged in masts and spars. 'I fancy,' wrote Nelson to Collingwood, 'if Emperors hear truth, that his fleet suffers more in a night than ours in a year.' Villeneuve's seamen lacked practice in handling their ships. When, in March, he well and truly escaped, he was a relieved man, but he was also disappointed, for the Spaniards at Cartagena did not join him, and he only managed to collect a few ships at Cadiz before speeding away for Martinique, believing Nelson was close behind him. Ganteaume, at Brest, had no luck at all. He was punched back into port by Cornwallis the moment he tried to put to sea, and Bonaparte forbade another attempt. Villeneuve would have to carry out the operation without the help of the other main French fleet.

The winds were foul for Nelson, and it was not until 6 May that he was even able to reach Gibraltar, far behind Villeneuve. He detached the *Royal Sovereign*, the only three-decked ship he had with him, except for the *Victory*, to protect a convoy with troops under Sir James Craig, destined for Malta, and then he stretched across the Atlantic in pursuit of the enemy. He was in greatly inferior strength to the force he could expect to encounter, and perhaps a wiser course would have been to head north to reinforce Cornwallis. But Nelson felt the compulsion of the chase, and he realized, better than most men of his time, the importance of protecting those West Indian islands he knew so well from his earlier commissions.

During the chase George Murray, reckoning the odds against them, which at one time were likely to be eleven sail of the line against twenty-two supposed to be with Villeneuve, observed to his chief: 'I suppose, my lord, that by packing all this canvas on the ships, your lordship means to engage the enemy, in case you come up with them.' 'Yes! By God, Murray, do I ...' was the admiral's terse reply.

The matter was not put to the test, for Nelson, misled by information given him by an army officer with whom he had once served, sought for Villeneuve off Trinidad, when, in actual fact, he was near Martinique. The Combined Fleet did, indeed, do some

175

Napoleon, a portrait
by Robert Lefevre.

RIGHT William Pitt, Prime Minister of
England, painted by Gainsborough.

176

harm to a convoy homeward-bound, taking fifteen sugar-laden ships, but the moment he knew Nelson was in the area of the Caribbean, Villeneuve raced back to Europe, and the bulk of the traffic, about 200 ships all told, was ensured of a safe passage.

Nelson sometimes referred to his ships as his 'wild geese'. At this time, the term was particularly appropriate. He himself was baffled and miserable, seeing nothing for it but to return to his station. At Gibraltar, he would at least be able to gather the latest news, and he would then proceed to England in the *Victory*, availing himself of the leave which he had received months earlier from the Admiralty.

There was plenty to hear, and more to surmise. Nelson anchored at Rosia Bay, Gibraltar, on 19 July, having outrun Villeneuve on his westerly course much as he had outrun Bruix years before in the Mediterranean. But he had despatched the recently captured corvette, *Curieux*, to England with such information as he possessed. The youthful captain, George Bettesworth, with his fast ship, was able to do Lord Barham, the reigning First Lord, a notable service. On his way, he caught sight of the Combined Fleet, and was able to report its course. His reward was post rank, and the command of a frigate.

Barham was an old man, but he was a master of strategy. He gave immediate orders for Cornwallis to detach ten ships from the Channel Fleet. These were to combine with five others from off Rochefort and the force was to lie in wait for Villeneuve, whose progress was slow. The plan succeeded. The British, under Sir Robert Calder, encountered Villeneuve on 22 July off Cape Finisterre and drove the Combined Fleet into Vigo, with the loss of two Spanish ships taken in prize. Calder was elated: Barham was not; and the nation was disappointed. Calder had, in fact, done creditably, faced with superior numbers, but he had not engaged in a Nelsonic manner, clinging to the enemy until the Combined Fleet was seriously diminished as a cohesive force, regardless of his own losses. The simple fact was that the battles of St Vincent, Camperdown and the Nile had set a new standard. This, so Barham felt, had not been maintained.

When he heard about the action, on his way to England, Nelson wrote to Fremantle, who had sent him all the latest news and gossip:

I was in truth bewildered by the account of Sir Robert Calder's victory, together with the hearing that John Bull was not content, which I am sorry for. Who can, my dear Fremantle, command all the success which our Country may wish? We have fought together and therefore well know what it is. I have had the best disposed Fleet of friends, but who can say what will be the event of a Battle, and it most sincerely grieves me, that in any of the papers it should be insinuated, that Lord Nelson could have done better. I should have fought the Enemy; so did my friend Calder; but who can say that he will be more successful than another? I only wish to stand upon my own merits, and not by comparison, one way or the other, upon the conduct of a Brother Officer . . .'.

Nelson arrived back in England on 18 August. Next day, he hauled down his flag, and sped to Merton. On the 20th, Villeneuve made a half-hearted attempt to steer to face Cornwallis, but then ran south for Cadiz. His arrival was watched by a detachment under Collingwood, one of whose smaller ships narrowly evaded capture. Five days later still, when Bonaparte learnt of the failure of his plans for his Fleet, he broke up his camp at Boulogne, and marched against the Austrians. For the time at least, invasion had been defeated.

There remained the Combined Fleet to be disposed of satisfactorily. The morale in the ships was low, but Collingwood wrote:

. . . they entered Cadiz with 36 sail — twenty seven or twenty eight of the line, and are in the port like a forest. I reckon them now to be 36 sail of the line [including ships already there] and plenty of frigates. What can I do with such a host? But I hope I shall get a reinforcement, suited to the occasion, and if I do, well betide us.

Collingwood had not long to wait, for Nelson was only twenty-five days in England. His time was divided between London and Merton. Although his cruise had been unsuccessful, and Barham had sent for *Victory*'s log to try to determine why, he was soon satisfied with Nelson's dispositions, and Nelson was asked to resume service as soon as possible, by Pitt as well as by the Admiralty. This, despite the attractions of home, fell in with his own inclinations. For he had not completed the task assigned to him, and when, on the early morning of 2 September, Captain Blackwood of the frigate *Euryalus* called at Merton, Nelson guessed his errand. 'I am sure you bring news of the French and Spanish fleets,' he said, 'and I think I shall yet have to beat them.'

By an extraordinary chance, Nelson and the future Duke of Wellington met, for the one and only time, during Nelson's last day in London. Both men were tanned by wind and sun, for both had just returned from very long spells at sea. Wellington, who was then a major-general aged thirty-six, and already the victor in a

series of campaigns in India, had landed at Dover from the *Trident* only the day before, and had speeded at once to the capital. The pair met in a waiting-room at the Colonial Office on 12 September, where they both had appointments with Castlereagh, who was Secretary for War and the Colonies. Wellington recognized Nelson at once, but the admiral did not know the younger man, and he began a conversation in his least attractive vein, all about himself and his achievements.

At last, made thoughtful by some remark of Wellington's, he left the room abruptly, to find out the general's name. When he returned, his whole attitude was different. Many years later, Wellington told John Wilson Croker, later Secretary of the Admiralty:

... all that I had thought a charlatan style had vanished, and he talked of the state of the country and of the aspect and probabilities of affairs on the Continent with a good sense, and a knowledge of subjects both at home and abroad, that surprised me equally and more agreeably than the first part of our interview had done; in fact, he talked like an officer and a statesman. The Secretary of State kept us long waiting, and certainly, for the last half or three quarters of an hour, I don't know that I ever had a conversation that interested me more.

Before he left Merton on his way to Trafalgar, Nelson gave Horatia (*opposite*) this silver gilt cup (*below*).

181

8 Trafalgar

WHERE FAMOUS PEOPLE are concerned, history and legend so often blend in course of time that it becomes hard to distinguish what is literally true and what are embellishments. Trafalgar is a classic instance, perhaps the fullest ever recorded, of how every fact and circumstance seemed as if it was part of an ordered pattern, as in a play of Sophocles or Shakespeare.

Nelson returned to Merton after his interview with Castlereagh and his talk with the future Duke of Wellington to take farewell of Emma and the child Horatia, for he was to sail immediately. He was tense. A West-Indian fortune teller, so he once told his sister Catherine, had caused him foreboding. He had had so many narrow escapes before, was by this time so battered, that he could never have thought himself as being among those whom bullets will never hit. Once, some years earlier, he had actually noted down on a slip of paper:

> *Wounds received by Lord Nelson:*
> His Eye in Corsica
> His Belly off Cape St Vincent
> His Arm at Teneriffe
> His Head in Egypt
> Tolerable for one War

It is hard to conceive of any admiral other than Nelson solemnly keeping by him a tally such as this, but Nelson, individual in so many ways, always had the artist's urge to record, and the habit, which he cultivated, remained strong. He kept a running diary on his last operation, and actually made an extra copy. Conscious of posterity, he did not wish to run the risk of his thoughts being lost to memory, and if one thing is more certain than another, it is that in 1805 he felt a 'march with destiny'. He had already had the experience of his original Nile despatch being captured by the French, and had ever since blessed his own forethought in sending a duplicate home by an alternative route.

The Trafalgar diary began in the high strain with which it was to finish. The date was 13 September, and it was a Friday too, which most sailors would have thought ominous.

... at half past Ten drove from dear Merton where I left all which hold dear in this World to go and serve my King and Country. May the Great God whom I adore enable me to fulfil the expectations of my Country and if it is His good pleasure that I should return, my thanks will never cease being offered up to the throne of His Mercy. If it is His good providence to cut short my days upon Earth I bow with the greatest submission

PREVIOUS PAGES The *Victory* rakes the Spanish.

OPPOSITE *Statement of wounds* – inventoried by Nelson for an admirer.

184

Wounds received by Lord Nelson

His Eye in Corsica
His Belly off Cape St Vincent
His arm at Teneriffe
His Head in Egypt—
Tolerance for One War

Written in 1803, by Lord Nelson,
at the request of a gentleman
who wished to have a state-
-ment of his wounds—

relying that He will protect those so dear to me that I may leave behind. His will be done amen amen amen.

Nelson embarked from Portsmouth, being joined by two politicians, George Canning, Treasurer of the Navy, and George Rose, Vice President of the Board of Trade, a friend of long standing. Hardy was on board to welcome him, and in the absence of George Murray would act as Captain of the Fleet. He had recently been on leave in Dorsetshire, his own part of the world, where he had had a conversation with the King, who was spending part of the summer at Weymouth. Canning and Rose dined with Nelson, who could have considered himself up to date with the latest news and gossip from home and abroad. The politicians, for their part, would have heard how Nelson hoped to fight Villeneuve, for it was no secret.

He had demonstrated it to Lord Sidmouth on a dining-room table; explained it to Captain Keats of the *Superb* in conversation one day at Merton; and a memorandum on the subject had been circulated to some of his officers. He wished above all things to avoid an indecisive battle in the old, unsatisfactory style, his aim being annihilation of the opposing fleet. His plan was to use three columns, one under his own direction, the other under that of his second in command, and a third, made up of fast ships, forming a reserve, to be employed as he decided. With his two principal lines, so he told Keats, 'I shall go at them at once, if I can, about one third of their Line from the leading Ship'.

'What do you think of it?' Nelson asked eagerly. Keats paused for consideration, and Nelson quickly followed up with – 'But I'll tell you what *I* think of it. I think it will surprise and confound the Enemy! They won't know what I am about. It will bring forward a pell-mell Battle, and that is what I want.'

In the event, Nelson did not have enough suitable ships for a third column, and if he was to confound the enemy, it would not be through surprise, for Villeneuve had learnt of Nelson's proposed tactics, and discussed them with his staff. 'He will try to double our rear, cut through the line, and bring against the ships thus isolated, groups of his own,' he wrote. 'Captains must rely on their courage and love of glory, rather than the signals of the admiral, who may already be engaged and wrapped up in smoke. The Captain who is not in action is not at his post.' Villeneuve was anticipating just such a 'pell-mell battle' as Nelson wished for, and his intention was not unlike that of his opponent.

The *Victory* sailed on Sunday 15 September, with the *Euryalus* in company. Blackwood, who would be in charge of the inshore frigates when Nelson reached his station, was one of the smartest men in the service, much approved by Nelson for his earlier conduct in the Mediterranean.

There was some danger, as it would have seemed, that Nelson might have to anchor off Weymouth. If so, he would be obliged to pay his respects to his sovereign. Highly as his professional merits were viewed, he was not in favour at Court by reason of the irregularity of his private life. In the event, Nelson escaped the trial of an audience, but he had written to Emma that, should he be forced to meet the King, 'I shall act as a man and your Nelson, neither courting nor ashamed to hold up my head before the greatest monarch in the world. I have, thank God, nothing to be ashamed of.'

On 18 September, Nelson sent Blackwood in to Plymouth to summon the *Ajax* and the *Thunderer*, two 74-gun ships appointed to his command. The same night he made all possible sail, leaving England astern. Ten days later, off the Rock of Lisbon, he wrote: 'sent *Euryalus* to join Vice Adl. Collingwood with my orders to put himself under Command, considering myself as within the Limits of my Command.' Blackwood had orders that when Nelson joined the rest of the fleet, the gun salute appropriate to a Commander-in-Chief was not to be fired. Nelson did not wish the enemy to know he had arrived, and, indeed, he was careful, throughout the weeks that followed, to keep the flag-ship out to sea. He did not favour a close watch, with the hostile coast in sight of the main body of his ships. His purpose was to tempt the enemy. All the same, he permitted himself one glimpse of their strength. After he joined Collingwood, on 28 September, he 'saw the Enemy's fleet in Cadiz amounting to 35 or 36 sail of the Line'. Actually, Villeneuve had thirty-three effective ships, and from the time the *Euryalus* was off the Spanish port, every movement he made would be reported by Blackwood.

It was no ready-made 'band of brothers' among whom Nelson had arrived. Only eight captains had served with him before, and all were restive under Collingwood. That stern man, who never spared himself, had forbidden visiting, and veterans like Fremantle, who now commanded the three-decked *Neptune*, wrote home in exasperation that they longed for a freer intercourse to lighten their tedious duties. Nelson's first business was to transform the spirit of the fleet. This was easy. His mere presence was a tonic and a reassurance, and when he encouraged socialities and

187

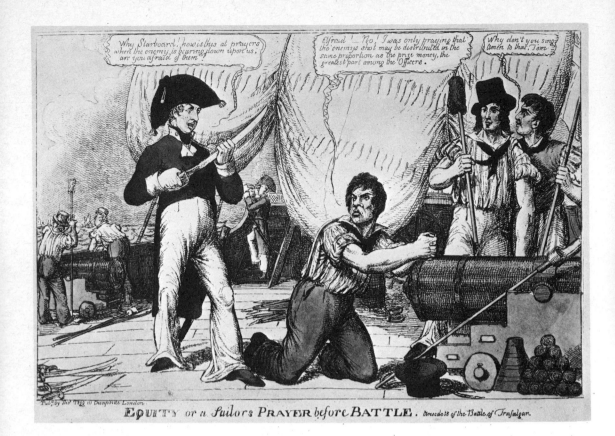

Why Starboard! how is this at prayers when the enemy is bearing down upon us, are you afraid of them?

Afraid! No, I was only praying that the enemys shot may be distributed in the same proportion as the prize money, the greatest part among the Officers.

Why don't you sing Amen to that, Tom?

Pub.d by Tho.s Tegg in Cheapside London

EQUITY or a Sailors PRAYER before BATTLE. Anecdote of the Battle of Trafalgar.

The proportion of prize money given to seamen was ludicrous in comparison to that paid to officers. A captain at Trafalgar received £973, while seamen and marines were given £1 17s 6d.

openly explained his ideas as to how he proposed to fight the expected battle, everything altered for the better.

'The reception I met with on joining the Fleet,' he wrote to a friend, 'caused the sweetest sensation of my life.' To Emma, on 1 October, he was still more explicit.

I believe my arrival was most welcome, not only to the Commander [Collingwood] but also to every individual in it, and when I came to explain the '*Nelson touch*' [the tactics he had expounded to Keats] it was like an electric shock. Some shed tears, all approved – 'It was new – it was singular – it was simple!' and, from Admirals downwards, it was repeated – 'It must succeed, if ever they will allow us to get at them! You are, my Lord, surrounded by friends whom you inspire with confidence.'

This was the spirit of the Nile. To those hitherto unaware of Nelson's methods, above all his trust in subordinates and his eagerness that they should use their initiative, it would have been

188

nothing short of revelation. No admiral, at least since the time of Hawke, had extended such ordered liberty, and done so with such touching assurance that it would be justified. That was what won hearts.

Nelson's attitude differed entirely from that of Collingwood, so it was a double blessing that they were devoted friends of very long standing. No subordinate could possibly have been more welcoming, so without jealousy, or such a rock of solidarity on which to build. There were three other admirals with the fleet – Sir Robert Calder, who was shortly to go home to face the enquiry, for which he had asked, about the conduct of his July battle; Thomas Louis, a favourite and favoured Nelsonian, whose ship was short of supplies, and who would have to be detached to Gibraltar to replenish, and Lord Northesk, a pupil of Rodney with whom Nelson had no previous acquaintance. Northesk's flag-ship was the veteran *Britannia*, a dull sailer, but he himself soon won Nelson's approval.

Collingwood and his chief continued their old terms of affectionate intimacy. On 9 October, Nelson noted that he had sent his second in command what the pair of them knew as the 'Nelson Trunk', a box to which each had a key. By means of this they could exchange memoranda, notes and papers. Collingwood thought little of his flag-captain, Rotheram, though he was a fellow Northumbrian, and Nelson did what he could to lighten the relationship by inviting them both to dinner. It did not soften Collingwood, but it helped to restore in Rotheram some of the confidence which his admiral was undermining. Collingwood liked to see to everything himself. His flag-captains were apt to be lonely creatures, and much criticized.

On 13 October, who should join the fleet but Sir Edward Berry, commanding Nelson's beloved *Agamemnon*. The old ship had been well seen to since her mishap at Copenhagen, but lacked something of her former turn of speed. 'Here comes Berry,' said Nelson gaily when his friend came in sight. '*Now* we shall have a battle!' His belief that the Combined Fleet would put to sea was not shared by all his officers. It was Napoleon himself who decided the matter by ordering Villeneuve into the Mediterranean, making doubly certain he complied by sending a senior officer to supersede him.

Berry, never the most alert of captains, had had a narrow escape on his way south. He had been chased by a three-decker and five two-decked French ships. Even when among his own people, it sometimes took perseverance to make him acknowledge signals.

CK *previous to the* BATTLE *of* TRAFALGAR.

His officers gathered round him, Nelson explains his plan of attack before Trafalgar.

Nelson was always able to rely more on his courage than his efficiency.

The same day that the *Agamemnon* appeared, Calder departed for home in his flag-ship, the *Prince of Wales*. It was a magnanimous gesture on Nelson's part to let this powerful vessel go, but he knew Calder might be in trouble, and could not bear to order him to transfer to a frigate, as the Admiralty wished. The wisdom of such a decision was highly doubtful, considering that the enemy had superior numbers. The generosity was exceptional, for Calder had never been close, and both Nelson and Collingwood, who had discussed his situation, thought Calder overbearing in his attitude to criticism.

Louis had already been sent off to Gibraltar with the five ships which most needed supplies, and he would escort a convoy as far as Cartagena. He complained bitterly that he would miss the battle. Nelson tried to reassure him that he would be back in time to take part in it, but Louis was right. By 14 October, Nelson had with him the twenty-seven ships of the line, and the two admirals, Collingwood and Northesk, with which he would fight Villeneuve.

Four days later, Nelson noted, 'fine weather, wind easterly, the Combined fleets cannot have finer Weather to put to sea'. Villeneuve felt the same, and as he was pressed by his own Government to do so, he had little choice, however much some of the French and Spanish captains felt the action to be misguided. Winter would soon be upon them, and they might have lain snug in harbour.

The first move which led to the encounter came on 19 October, when Nelson recorded: 'the *Mars*, being one of the look out ships, made the signal that the Enemy were coming out of Port. Made the signal for a general chase south east.' Six hours later, the *Colossus* reported that the Combined Fleet was actually at sea, and heading for the Straits of Gibraltar. Nelson signalled to Blackwood that he relied on his keeping sight of the enemy while his scattered ships assembled into the two prescribed columns, taking stations 'as convenient'. Such a free and easy procedure would have been anathema to a more rigid commander, and indeed one of the Trafalgar captains stated afterwards that they all 'scrambled into battle as best they could'. Nelson noted with approval that 'the frigates and Look out ships kept sight of the Enemy most admirably all night and told me by Signals which tack they were upon'.

On 21 October, a day memorable in his family since it was that upon which Maurice Suckling had made his name in the *Dread-*

nought, Nelson made the entry in his Diary which has become part of the treasury of the language.

May the Great God whom I worship Grant to my Country and for the benefit of Europe in General a great and Glorious Victory, and may no misconduct in any one tarnish it, and May humanity after Victory be the predominant feature in the British fleet. For myself individually I commit my Life to Him who made me, and may his blessing light upon my endeavours for serving my Country faithfully, to Him I resign myself and the Just cause which is entrusted to me to Defend –

Amen, Amen, Amen.

There followed a codicil leaving 'Emma, Lady Hamilton ... a Legacy to my King and Country that they will give her an ample provision to maintain her Rank in Life. . . . To the beneficence of my Country my adopted daughter Horatia Nelson Thompson. . . .'

It is a reflection on the pace at which the preliminaries to battle in the days of sail warfare were sometimes conducted that on a day of light airs, but with the enemy in sight, Nelson could make an extended entry into his diary, copy it out, settle his affairs, inspect and approve the arrangements of his flag-ship, and still have time to attend to essential signals and instructions. Such conditions imply a confidence and an orderliness to which neither Villeneuve nor his Spanish colleagues, Gravina and d'Alava, could aspire.

Villeneuve's heart failed him before he reached the Straits. His fleet had been weeks in harbour, and its manœuvring had never been good. When he sighted the British, who were slowly forming into their respective columns, he decided to reverse course and to return to Cadiz. He would have the excuse that the enemy were in greater strength than he had supposed, and that the Emperor had not enjoined him to accept battle except on favourable terms. His decision came too late. As the signal went up on his flag-ship, the *Bucentaure*, Commodore Churraca, on board the *San Juan Nepomuceno*, which now became the rear ship of a ragged line, turned to his second in command and said: 'The Fleet is doomed. The French admiral does not understand his business. He has compromised us all.' Churraca had been leading the fleet, and his point was that Villeneuve would have had a better chance of survival by holding to his original course, even if the fighting became a chase. As it was, since he could not hope to regain safety under existing weather conditions, and as the wind was in Nelson's favour, a 'pell-mell battle' was unavoidable. When it took place, superior seamanship, gunnery and experience would lead to disaster.

Victory Oct^r: 19: 1805
Noon Cadiz E^tE 16 Leagues

My Dearest beloved Emma the dear
friend of my bosom the Signal has
been made that the Enemys Combined
fleet are coming out of Port, We
have very little Wind so that I have
no hopes of seeing them before to morrow
may the God of Battles crown my
Endeavours with success at all events
I will take care that my name shall ever
be most dear to you and Horatia both
of whom I love as much as my own
life, and as my last writing before the
battle will be to you so I hope in God that
I shall live to finish my letter after the

Battle, may heaven bless you prays
Your Nelson & Bronté, Octr. 20th in the
morning we were close to the mouth of the
Streights but the Wind had not come far
enough to the Westward to allow the Combined
fleets to weather the Shoals of Trafalgar but
they were counted as far as forty Sail of Ships
of War which I suppose to be 34 of the Line
and Six frigates, a Group of them was
seen off the Lighthouse of Cadiz this Morn^g
but it blows so very fresh I think Weather
that I rather believe they will go into
the Harbour before night, May God
almighty give us success over these fellows

Nelson's last letter to Emma, found unfinished on his desk after the battle and taken to Emma by Captain Hardy. Emma has added a moving inscription on the last page.

194

and enable us to get a Peace

This letter was found open on
his desk & brought to
Lady Hamilton by
Capn Hardy

oh miserable wretched
Emma
oh glorious & happy Nelson

... At 8 Observed the British Flat forming their Line the head most Ships
from the Enemys enter 8 & 9 Miles the Enemys force consist of Thirty
three Sail the Line five Frigates and two Brigs light Winds & hazy with
a great Swell from the Wesw. English Flat all Sail set Standing towards
the Enemy them on the Starboard Tack at 8 — & answd. Lord Nelsens Sigl
for Captain Blackwood and went immediatly on Board the Victory, took
our Station on the Victorys Larboard Quarter and repeated the Admirals
Sigl at 10 observed the Enemy wearing and comming to the Wind on
the Larboard Tack at 11 — 40 repeated Lord Nelsens Telegraph Message
I intend to push or go through the end of the Enemys Line to
prevent them getting in to Cadiz Saw the Land bearing ENE 5 & 6 Leagues
At 11 — 56 repeated Lord Nelsens Telegraph Message, England
expects that every Man will do his Duty At Noon light Winds and
a great Swell from the Wesw. Observed the Royal Sovereign (Admiral
Collingwood) leading the Lee Line bearing Down on the Enemys Rear Line
being then nearly within Gun Shot of them Lord Nelson leading the Weather
Line bore Down upon the Enemys center Captain Blackwood Left 12w
from the Victory Cape Trafalgar SEBE about 5 Leagues Left

Signals made &c on the 21st October 1805

H	M	H	M	By Whom	To Whom	No	H	M	H	M	By Whom	To Whom	No
1	50	"	"	Euryalus	Sirius	&c&c		7	"	"	Euryalus	Repeated from the Victory	13
1	55	"	"	Sirius	Euryalus	{32 Num.		7	40	"	Do	Do		7 6 East
2	"	"	"	Euryalus	Sirius	26		8	"	"	Victory	Euryalus	Captn.
2	10	"	"	Do	Do	5 & 394	Noon	"	Do	Repeated from the Victory	{63}grea
4	10	"	"	Do	Victory	413 North with 2 Gun							
4	20	"	"	Do	Naiad Phoebe }	100							
5	10	"	"	Do	Do	154 with 3 Guns							
5	25	"	"	Do	Do	18 North 1 Gun							
5	45	"	"	Do	Victory	362 5Guns							

LEFT John Pasco,
lieutenant aboard the
Victory at Trafalgar.

OPPOSITE The entry from
the log of the *Euryalus*
recording Nelson's immortal
'England expects that every
man will do his duty'.

Nelson ordered all his ships to fly his own squadronal flag as Vice Admiral of the White, with a Union flag suspended from the fore topgallant stay as an additional emblem. His signal 'England Expects that every Man will do his Duty' was hoisted a few minutes before noon, according to the log of the *Euryalus*. It had a cheerful reception, the remarks of the lower deck, that they had always done theirs and anyway had no choice in the matter, were not repeated in more exalted quarters.

Collingwood's line, led by the *Royal Sovereign*, was hotly engaged by midday. This was some time before fire from the *Victory* could be effective and gave Nelson the chance to exclaim in admiration – 'See how that noble fellow, Collingwood, carries his

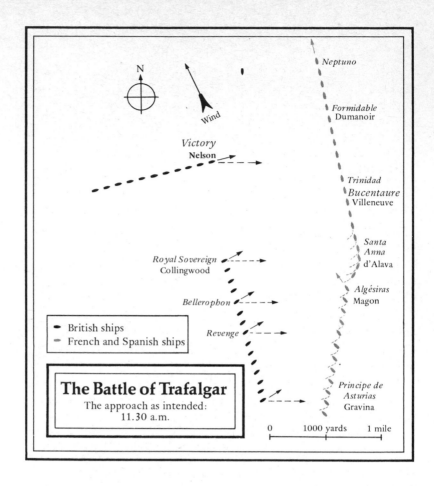

N

Wind

Victory
Nelson

Neptuno

Formidable
Dumanoir

Trinidad
Bucentaure
Villeneuve

Royal Sovereign
Collingwood

Santa
Anna
d'Alava

Bellerophon

Algésiras
Magon

Revenge

- British ships
- French and Spanish ships

The Battle of Trafalgar
The approach as intended:
11.30 a.m.

Principe de
Asturias
Gravina

0   1000 yards   1 mile

ship into action!' Collingwood's gunnery was always a model for the rest of the fleet. His last signal from Nelson was received a few minutes before his broadsides opened. It ran: 'I intend to push through the enemy's line to prevent them getting into Cadiz.' Collingwood is said to have remarked that he wished Nelson would stop signalling. Everyone knew exactly what they were supposed to do.

Collingwood, in a fast ship, fought alone till his supporting column could arrive, crowding all sail. The lee line was made up of 74s, apart from the *Royal Sovereign*. Valour would have to make up for size, for they would be opposed by far greater weight of metal. In Nelson's weather line, the admiral had packed his punch. The three leading ships were all three-deckers, and a fourth, the *Britannia*, was not far behind. All had heavy casualties. John Barclay, an acting lieutenant in the *Britannia*, who had recently

198

been transferred from the *Victory*, in which he had served as a Master's Mate, entered in his Journal:

About $\frac{1}{4}$ before one Lord Nelson, after having sustained a most galling fire in running down, opened both sides of the *Victory* on the headmost ships of their centre division. He was close followed up by the *Temeraire*, *Neptune*, *Conqueror*, *Leviathian* and this Ship, and pushed thro' their line about the 14 from the Van. Several raking shot called forth our Exertions about 10 minutes after our Noble Chief.

Here began the Din of War . . .

That din continued until Nelson's work was done, and long after he had himself received a mortal wound. The admiral, conspicuous with the stars and medals on his uniform, was pacing the quarter-deck with Hardy, the *Victory* being then under heavy fire, when at about a quarter past one he was hit by a bullet fired from a fighting-top in the French ship *Redoutable*, which was then almost bilge to bilge alongside the *Victory*. Captain Lucas, the French commander, was an officer of outstanding zeal. He had trained his ship's company to be ready for anything; his discipline was exceptional, even after tremendously heavy casualties had been suffered, and Nelson was indeed unlucky to have come up against such an opponent.

The *Victory* had first engaged the *Bucentaure* herself, but Villeneuve's defence did not compare with that of Lucas, and in fact the Commander-in-Chief surrendered before the result of the battle was clear. Lucas, on the other hand, was actually prepared to board such a towering opponent as the British flag-ship. His attempt was beaten off, but with difficulty, and at the cost of the life of Captain Charles Adair of the Marines.

Nelson was carried below to the cockpit by Sergeant Secker and two seamen. 'They have done for me at last,' he said to his flag-captain. 'I hope not,' said Hardy, remembering Nelson's wound at the Nile, which he had thought at first to be mortal. 'Yes,' answered the admiral, 'my backbone is shot through.' He lived for several hours more, but in great pain, and with the certainty that nothing could be done to save him. Even the conduct of the battle was out of his hands. It was every captain for himself; but Nelson knew well enough he could rely on their success. There was a sentence in his tactical memorandum which all who read it would have remembered:

Captains are to look to their particular Line as their rallying point, but in case signals cannot be seen, or clearly understood, no captain can do very wrong if he places his ship alongside that of an enemy.

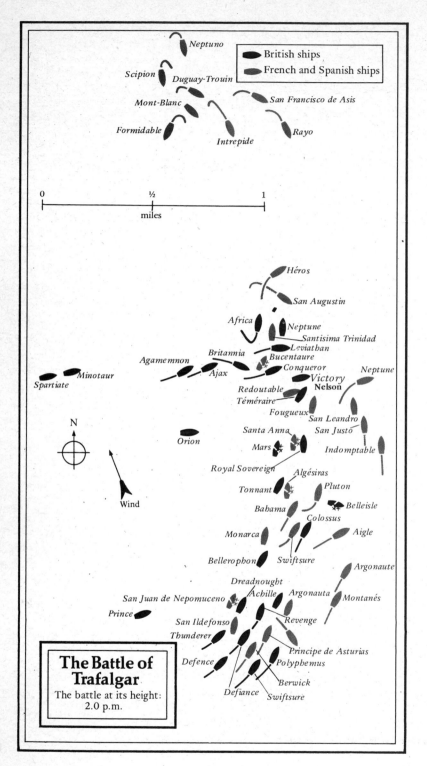

RIGHT First, second and third positions of the fleet at Trafalgar – a plan made by an officer aboard the *Euryalus*.

Neptuno

Scipion

Duguay-Trouin

Mont-Blanc

San Francisco de Asis

Formidable

Rayo

Intrepide

British ships
French and Spanish ships

0   ½   1

miles

Héros

San Augustin

Africa

Neptune

Santisima Trinidad

Leviathan

Britannia

Bucentaure

Agamemnon

Conqueror

Neptune

Ajax

Victory

Spartiate

Minotaur

Nelson

Redoutable

Téméraire

Fougueux

San Leandro

N

Orion

Santa Anna

San Justo

Mars

Indomptable

Royal Sovereign

Algésiras

Tonnant

Pluton

Wind

Bahama

Belleisle

Colossus

Monarca

Aigle

Bellerophon

Swiftsure

Argonaute

Dreadnought

Argonauta

San Juan de Nepomuceno

Achille

Montanés

Prince

Revenge

San Ildefonso

Thunderer

Principe de Asturias

The Battle of Trafalgar

Defence

Polyphemus

The battle at its height:
2.0 p.m.

Berwick

Defiance

Swiftsure

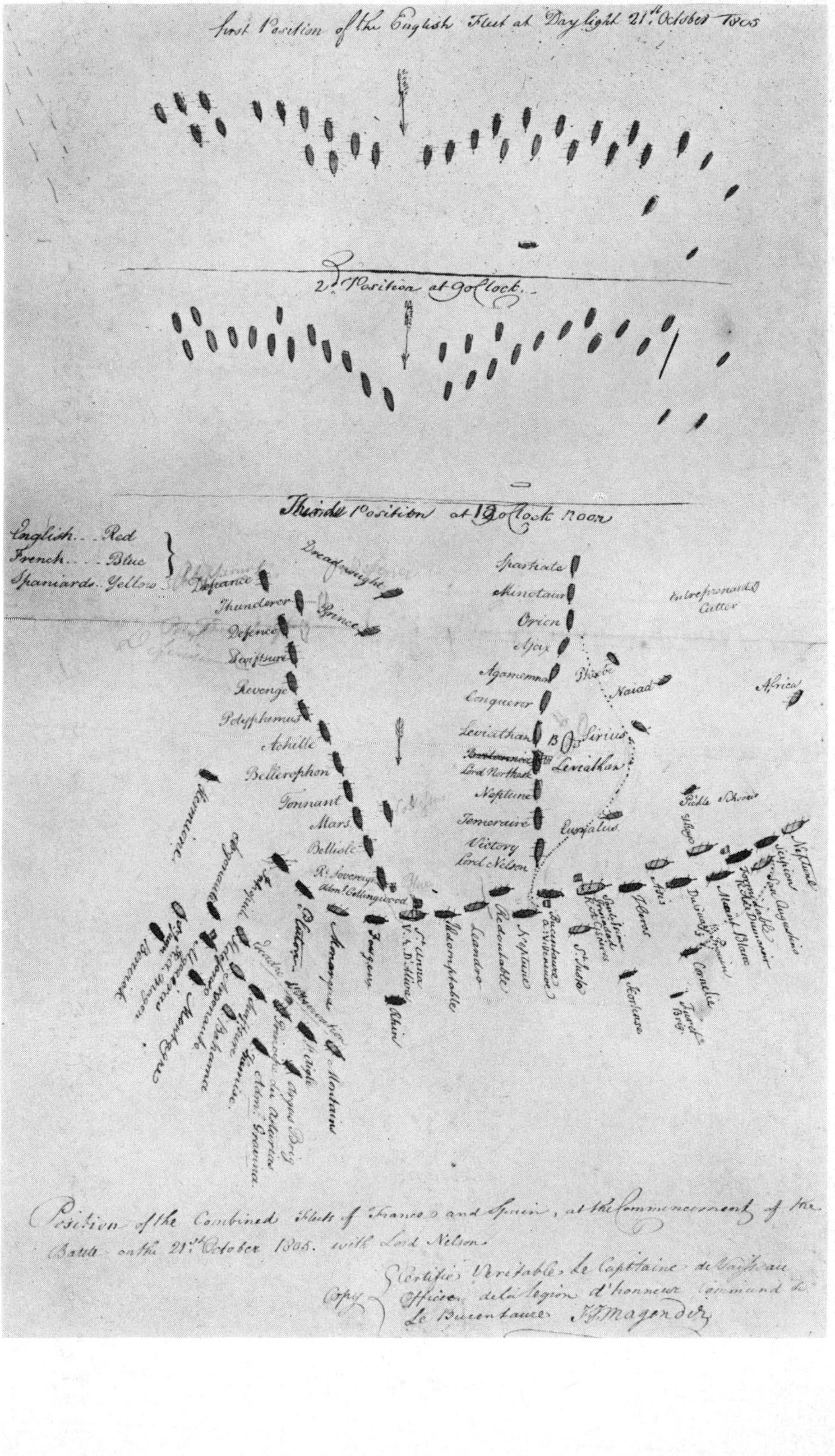

First Position of the English Fleet at Day Light 21st October 1805

2d Position at 9 oClock

Third Position at 12 oClock Noon

English....Red
French....Blue
Spaniards..Yellow

Defiance
Thunderer
Defence
Dreadnought
Prince
Revenge
Polyphemus
Achille
Bellerophon
Tonnant
Mars
Belisle
R. Sovereign Adm.l Collingwood

Spartiate
Minotaur
Orion
Ajax
Agamemnon
Conqueror
Leviathan
Britannia Lord Northesk
Neptune
Temeraire
Victory Lord Nelson

Phœbe
Naiad
Sirius
Leviathan
Euryalus

Intrepid Cutter
Africa

Position of the Combined Fleets of France and Spain, at the Commencement of the
Battle on the 21st October 1805. with Lord Nelson.

Certifié Véritable, Le Capitaine de Vaisseau
Copy   Officier de la Légion d'honneur Commandant
          Le Bucentaure J.F. Magendie

The battle of Trafalgar as
seen by an English (*right*)
and a Spanish artist (*below*).

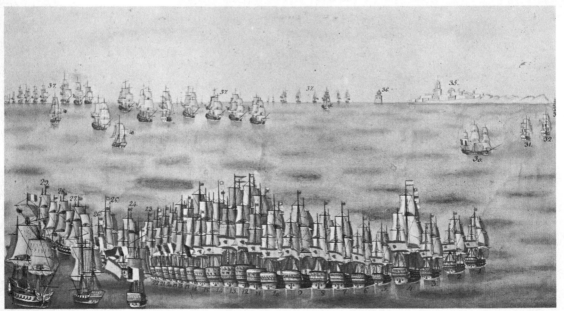

Such was the case in his fleet while Nelson lay dying, his thoughts continually ranging between the task he had begun so well, and the woman he loved. Hardy could not be spared from the upper deck except for short spells, but before Nelson died he was able to report that something very near annihilation had been achieved. Nelson thanked God he had done his duty; remarked how dear was life to all men, and about half past four sank into a state from which he did not recover.

The battle was not yet over, and there was a danger that some of the advanced enemy ships, then nearing Cadiz, which had not hitherto been engaged, would again reverse course in an attempt to help the rest. The threat was made, but countered. The French vessels made off, only to be snapped up a fortnight later by Sir Richard Strachan.

When Nelson died, Collingwood was one of the few men in the fleet, outside the *Victory*, who knew that the burden of command had fallen on him. Hardy had informed him by a message, sent in a boat through the shot-torn waters, that Nelson could not live. When darkness fell, his death was confirmed by the fact that the admiral's lantern, above the poop of the *Victory*, stayed unlit. But such were the weather conditions, and the battered and scattered state of the fleet, that even some of the captains who had been closest to the *Victory* during the battle, did not learn the portentous news for days.

Villeneuve was a prisoner-of-war, the Combined Fleet was broken as a cohesive force, but in the aftermath of the battle many ships were sunk or cast ashore. A storm, such as Nelson himself had predicted, arose in the evening, and his wish that the fleet should anchor could not be obeyed. Many ships had lost the necessary tackle; others were dismasted and in tow, and of the defeated forces, only four prizes were eventually brought into Gibraltar. A notably sad loss was that of the *Santissima Trinidada*, which had struck her colours and had a prize crew aboard. She had already had one narrow escape at St Vincent. She did not survive Trafalgar. She sank before the weary repair parties could plug the many holes below her water line. Even some of the British ships, including the *Victory* and *Royal Sovereign*, were in a dangerous state, though none were lost, and most were soon repaired and fully operational.

Collingwood transferred his flag immediately after the battle to the *Euryalus*. This was a deserved compliment to Blackwood, whose signal staff had done splendid work. It was from this frigate that

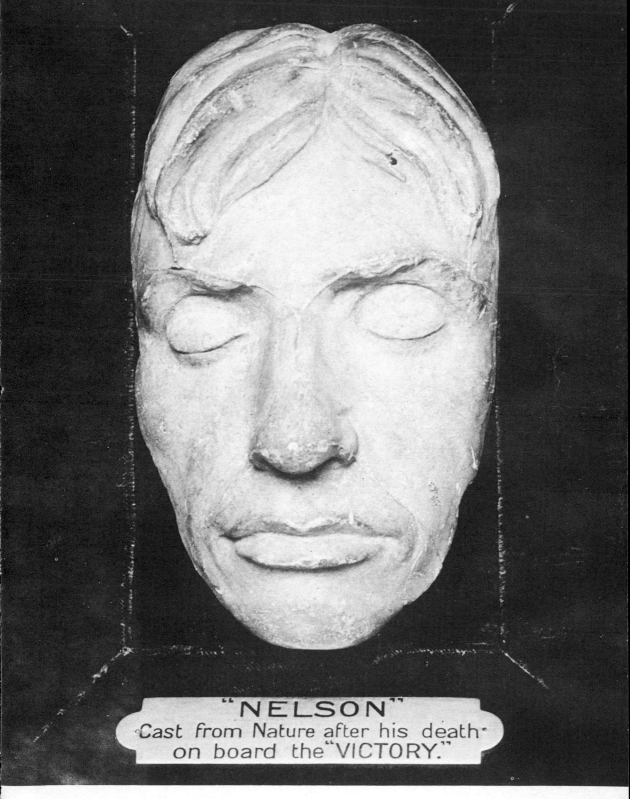

"NELSON"
Cast from Nature after his death
on board the "VICTORY."

BRITONS !

Your NELSON is dead!

Trust not in an Arm of Flesh, but in the *Living GOD!*

WHAT SAID THE BRAVE

Nelson, Duncan, Howe?

"GOD hath given us the VICTORY !"

His Arm is not cold in Death, nor shortened that it cannot Save.

BRITONS!

Fear GOD, Fear SIN, And Then

Fear Nothing.

Collingwood wrote the despatch which thrilled and saddened his countrymen. From it, he also addressed a General Order which in its generosity of spirit could have served as a pattern.

OPPOSITE This poster was probably published by a religious organization.

The ever-to-be lamented death of Lord Viscount Nelson, Duke of Brontë, the Commander-in-Chief, who fell in the action of the 21st, in the arms of Victory, covered with glory – whose name will be ever dear to the British Navy and the British Nation, whose zeal for the honour of his King, and for the interest of his Country, will be ever held up as a shining example for a British seaman – leaves me a duty to return my thanks to the Right Honourable Rear-Admiral, the Captains, Officers, Seamen and Detachments of Royal Marines, serving on board His Majesty's squadron, now under my command, for their conduct on that day.

But where can I find language to express my sentiments of the valour and skill which were displayed by the Officers, the Seamen and Marines, in the battle with the enemy, where every individual appeared a hero on whom the glory of his Country depended? The attack was irresistible, and the issue of it adds to the page of naval annals a brilliant instance of what Britons can do, when their King and Country need their service. . . .

At this distant day, when so many, sailors and civilians alike, have shared the bitter experience of war, such words may appear hackneyed or bombastic. They were not. They came from one who knew the full meaning of conflict, and they were what his audience hoped to receive. Collingwood wrote about the battle many times, with many variations, to correspondents high and low, but he never wrote as if it was a wearisome duty.

Considering that he had the whole management of the fleet, a task which occupied him continuously over the next five years, and which never permitted him to enjoy his home and family again, this was in itself wonderful. Nor did he ever so much as mention, except to his relations, that he had himself been wounded.

How Collingwood's behaviour struck George III, who scarcely knew him, was conveyed in a letter which the admiral regarded as 'the object of his life'. When the King read the report of the battle, he dictated a message.

Every tribute of praise appears to His Majesty due to Lord Nelson, whose loss he can never sufficiently regret; but His Majesty considers it very fortunate that the command, under circumstances so critical, should have devolved upon an officer of such consummate valour, judgement and skill, as Admiral Collingwood has proved himself to be, every part of whose conduct he considers deserving his entire approbation and admiration. . . .

207

A Hero's Funeral

Nelson's body lay in state in the
Painted Hall at Greenwich (*below*)
before a flotilla of small boats
accompanied his funeral barge up
river from Greenwich (*overleaf*) to
Whitehall. From here a vast
procession followed his elaborate
shiplike hearse to St Paul's
Cathedral. On the right is a diagram
of the procession.

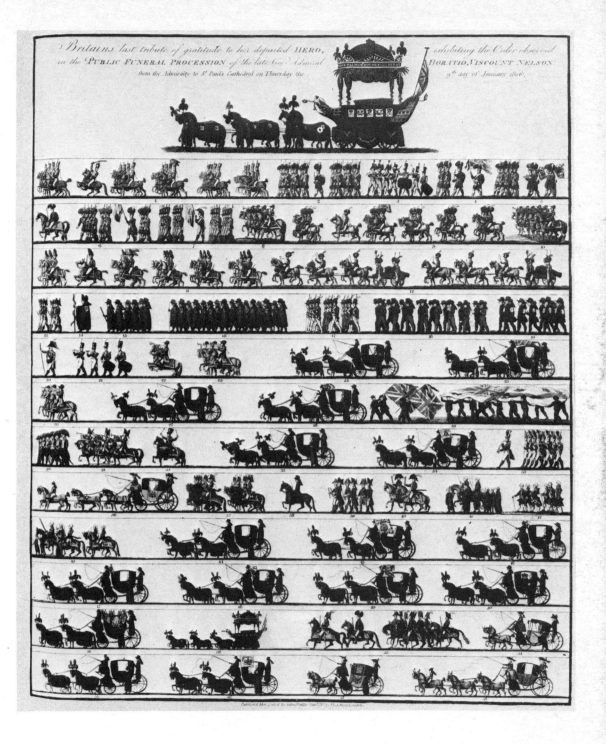

It was Alexander Ball who spoke of Nelson as a 'heaven-born admiral', an opinion which has been echoed ever since. Tributes came from near and far, and when news of Trafalgar reached London in November, widespread grief mingled with elation and pride at the achievement of the fleet. Much later in the century, Admiral Mahan, the American who has proved to be Nelson's most percipient biographer, called him 'the embodiment of sea power'. Although this leaves little more to be said, it may be valuable to record one more instance of a friend's appraisal. This was given by Collingwood in a letter he wrote in 1806 to Walter Spencer-Stanhope. It has since then become the property of the nation, and remained unpublished until 1966.

I have indeed had a severe loss in the death of my excellent friend Lord Nelson. Since the year '73 we have been on terms of the greatest intimacy. Chance has thrown us very much together in service, and on many occasions we have acted in concert. There is scarce a naval subject that has not been the subject of discussion, so that his opinions were familiar to me, and so firmly founded on principles of honour, of justice, of attachment to his Country, at the same time so entirely divested of everything interested to himself, that it was impossible to consider him but with admiration. He liked fame, he was open to flattery, so that people sometimes got about him, who were unworthy of him – he is a loss to his Country that cannot easily be replaced.

Each word was true, and Nelson never was replaced. The war against the French Empire was to continue for ten years after Trafalgar, but he had finally demonstrated the superiority of the British fleet. The Navy was indeed due for setbacks, particularly in a brief and unnecessary war with the United States which broke out in 1812, but Trafalgar was the last major fleet action to take place before Napoleon was lodged on St Helena, and before Europe could be re-ordered. When land power could be brought to the aid of sea-power, when Napoleon, by arrogance and misjudgement, aroused the nationalism of Spaniards and Germans, and exhausted an entire army against the illimitable spaces of Russia, he tempted fortune too much. 'Mark the end', Nelson had written across a copy of one of the Emperor's letters, in the certainty that one day he would over-reach himself.

Nelson's 'legacy' to his 'King and Country' was not attended to, and has ever since been a matter of concern. Emma Hamilton had many friends, but none in such powerful quarters as to ensure her 'an ample provision to maintain her Rank in Life'. In point of fact, Nelson and her husband had between them left her considerable means. The estate at Merton became her own. She had £800 a year under the terms of Sir William Hamilton's will (£100 of which went to her mother), Horatia had been left £4,000 by her father, and a prudent woman would have considered herself very comfortably off by the standards of the day, seeing that in addition to all this, Nelson added a capital sum of £2,000 and an annuity of £500 charged on the estate at Brontë in Sicily.

Alas, Emma was never prudent. She was incurably lavish with what she had, was already in debt, and had no dependable man of business at hand to guide her affairs. She slid downhill with increasing momentum and ceaseless complaint, dying at Calais in 1815 from the effects of drink. Horatia was afterwards well taken care of by Nelson's relations. She married happily, and in later years came to look startlingly like her father.

News of Nelson's death was sent to the neglected Fanny in a considerately worded letter from Lord Barham, and she received a life pension of £2,000 a year to console her for the years in the

BELOW A gold locket engraved with Nelson's codicil to his will leaving Lady Hamilton as a 'legacy to my King and Country'.

The Death of Nelson
by Arthur Devis.

The Immortal Memory

The public adoration felt for Nelson was catered for by the manufacture, after his death, of innumerable mementos such as this jug and these snuffboxes. A medal (*far right*) was given to those who had served at Trafalgar by Nelson's prize agent.

A detailed diagram of the ball which killed Nelson.

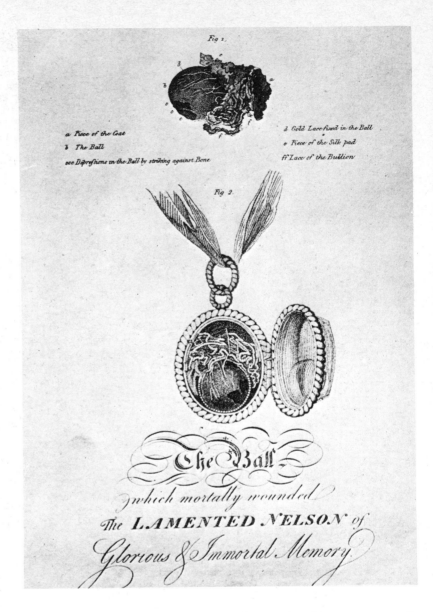

Fig 1.

a Piece of the Coat
b The Ball
ccc Depressions in the Ball by striking against Bone

d Gold Lace fixed in the Ball
e Piece of the Silk pad
ff Lace of the Bullion

Fig 2.

The Ball

which mortally wounded

The LAMENTED NELSON of

Glorious & Immortal Memory

shadows. She remained devoted to her husband's memory until her death in 1831, and in her later years even Nelson's most bigoted partisans looked upon her as a much wronged woman.

Nelson's eldest surviving brother William, by what Collingwood aptly described as one of Dame Fortune's 'frisks', was the undeserving object of the nation's bounty. He was already a Prebendary of Canterbury, an appointment he had received as a favour to the admiral. He became an Earl, was endowed with a

pension of £5,000 a year, and given the sum of £99,000 with which to purchase a landed estate. Collingwood was also made a peer, but his modest and reasonable request that his title should descend through his daughters, since he had no sons, was not attended to. Hardy became a baronet, and the ship's company of the *Victory*, released at last from his terrible discipline, found themselves popular heroes. They were a main attraction at Nelson's elaborate funeral at St Paul's, after the flag-ship reached home.

The widowed Lady Nelson, neglected during his later life, honoured his memory for the rest of her life.

219

The cult of Nelson has continued, and it has swollen into an industry almost as ramified as that of Shakespeare. A century after Trafalgar, learned commentators set to work to analyse the battle, perhaps in the hope of unravelling the secret of Nelson's tactics. They could have spared their pains, for the pith of the matter lay in Nelson's ability to seize whatever opportunities came his way, without regard to rules, precedents or tradition, and to squeeze the last ounce out of what was offered.

His legacy to the Navy he adorned could have been the memory of how much could be achieved by giving subordinates every encouragement to exercise initiative within a general framework of strategic objectives and tactical principles. In fact, his shining example led to complacency, and the freedom of action which he himself had exercised and fostered was never sufficiently encouraged. British seamen continued to believe themselves unequalled in their own profession, and it took a succession of shocks, administered during the two great wars of the present century, to make their leaders properly aware of the truth that although thought and responsibility is a painful business (as Rodney once remarked to his captains), yet without application, subtlety, adaptability, full appreciation of the capabilities of an opponent, and a disregard of unnecessary rules, failure may result, and the price of failure may be extinction.

Sources
and Bibliography

The manuscript sources of material for the biography of Nelson, including documentation in the British Museum, the National Maritime Museum, Greenwich, and the Nelson Museum, Monmouth, are very considerable and still provide scope for research, as do the logs of the ships which Nelson commanded, or in which he flew his flag, now in the Public Record Office.

A useful survey of such sources appeared in the *Mariner's Mirror*, the Journal of the Society for Nautical Research. This was compiled by Miss K.F.Lindsay-MacDougall and is to be found in the volume covering the year 1955 (pp. 227–32). A small but important recent addition is a series of letters from Collingwood, one of which is quoted herein, now British Museum Add. MSS 52780.

The principal printed material in book form, including the important biographies by Alfred Mahan (1897) and Carola Oman (1947) is listed and annotated in *Lord Nelson: a Guide to Reading* (Caravel Press: 1955), which was issued by the present writer and which contains a brief note on contemporary portraits.

The main source of printed record is comprised in the 7 volumes of the *Dispatches and Letters of Lord Viscount Nelson*, edited by Sir Harris Nicolas (Colburn: 1845-6). A substantial supplement to this work, including fuller texts of material first printed by Nicolas, is the volume edited by George P.B.Naish, *Nelson's Letters to his Wife and other Documents, 1785-1831* (Navy Records Society and Routledge and Kegan Paul: 1958).

Since Naish's work, the following studies of Nelson have appeared, and the Nelson industry is such that it cannot claim to be inclusive:

Oliver Warner, *A Portrait of Lord Nelson*, Chatto and Windus, 1958.
Dudley Pope, *England Expects*, Weidenfeld and Nicolson, 1959.
Oliver Warner, *Nelson's Battles*, Batsford, 1965.
Russell Grenfell, *Horatio Nelson*, Faber, 1968. (A revision of *Nelson the Sailor*, 1949, under a new title.)
Tom Pocock, *Nelson and his World*, Thames and Hudson, 1968.
Dudley Pope, *The Great Gamble: Nelson at Copenhagen*, Weidenfeld and Nicolson, 1972.

Geoffrey Bennett, *Nelson the Commander*, Batsford, 1972.

Oliver Warner, *Nelson's Last Diary and the Prayer before Trafalgar*, Seeley Service, 1972.

Christopher Lloyd, *Nelson and Sea Power*, English Universities Press, 1973.

Roy Hattersley, *Nelson*, Weidenfeld and Nicolson, 1974.

NOTE I am indebted to Captain H.L.Cryer RN for kindly allowing me to make use of information concerning James Carse of HMS *Boreas* which he published in the *Mariner's Mirror*, February 1974.

List of Illustrations

Index

Mutine, 95, 112

Naples, 50–3, 96, 104, 109, 116, 165
Napoleon Bonaparte, 54, 96, 97, 104, 131, 147, 160, 162, 172, 173, 174, 179, 189, 212
navy: discipline, 20–1, 163–172; life for the privileged, 172–3; diet, 173
Naval Chronicle, 12, 81
Nelson, Catherine (sister), 12, 31, 184
Nelson, Edmund (father), 12, 45, 151
Nelson, Fanny (wife), 42, 85, 87, 88, 121, 126, 150, 158, 213, 218
Nelson, Horatia (daughter), 126, 150, 158, 184, 193, 213
Nelson, Horatio: character, 12, 31, 134, 180;
joins navy, 13;
acting lieutenant of *Worcester*, 25;
in West Indies, 28;
made post captain, 28;
expedition against Spaniards in Nicaragua, 29;
meeting with Prince William Henry, 34–5;
marriage to Fanny, 42;
farming, 46;
in Naples, 53;
Corsican campaign, 56;
blinded in one eye, 57;
made Colonel of Marines, 61;
first achieves public acclaim, 68;
Cape St Vincent, 69–77;
withdrawal from Elba, 81;

attacks Santa Cruz, Teneriffe and loses arm, 82–5;
at the Nile, 98–103;
receives peerage, 103;
receives title of Brontë, 118;
birth of Horatia, 126;
at Copenhagen, 130–42;
made commander-in-chief of the British Fleet, 145;
on shore 1801–3, 158–62;
meets Wellington, 180;
embarks for Trafalgar, 186;
mortally wounded, 199;
appraisal of career, 212, 220
Nelson, Maurice (brother), 30
Nelson, Susanna (sister), 31
Nelson, William (brother), 30, 31, 38, 218–19
Neptune, 187, 199
Nicolas, Sir Harris, 12
Nisbet, Frances, *see* Fanny Nelson
Nisbet, Josiah (Nelson's stepson), 42, 50, 53, 54, 57, 60, 85, 86, 94, 109, 150, 158
Nore, 81
Northesk, Lord, 192
Northumberland, 121
Norway, 127

Orde, Sir John, 94
Orfordness, 147
L'Orient, 98, 99, 102
Orion, 94, 95

Palermo, 109, 118
Paoli, General, 56
Parker, Sir Hyde, 126, 127, 130, 133, 139, 142, 145, 146, 147
Parker, Admiral Sir Peter, 28, 47

Penelope, 121
Pérée, Rear Admiral, 121
Pitt, William, the Younger, 104, 127, 149, 174, 179
Plymouth, 122, 126, 187
Port Mahon, 56, 88, 118
Port Royal, 29, 30
Portsmouth, 186
Portugal, 88
Prince of Wales, 192
Prussia, 127

Raisonable, 13, 16
Rathbone, John, 16
Redoutable, 199
Remonier, Louis, 85
Riou, Captain, 135
Rose, George, 186
Rotheram, Captain, 189
Royal Sovereign, 175, 197, 198, 204
Ruffo, Cardinal, 116
Russell, 134
Russia, 104, 127, 133, 139, 142, 146

St George, 126
St Omer, 38, 94
St Petersburg, 146
St Vincent, Earl of, *see* Jervis, Sir John
Salvador del Mundo, 73
San Isidro, 73
San Josef, 22, 73, 126
San Juan Nepomuceno, 193
San Nicholas, 73
Santa Cruz, Teneriffe, 82
Santissima Trinidada, 72, 73, 204
Sardinia, 55, 94